TIGER

TIGER
— PORTRAIT OF A PREDATOR —

VALMIK THAPAR

PHOTOGRAPHS BY
GÜNTER ZIESLER
— AND —
FATEH SINGH RATHORE

FOREWORD BY
RAJIV GANDHI, PRIME MINISTER OF INDIA

COLLINS
8 Grafton Street, London W1
1986

To Genghis and F.S., both masters
of the field

FRONTISPIECE
In the blistering heat of summer, the tigress Noon rests by a
water-hole, partially shaded by a rock face festooned with
creepers and the tangled roots of banyan trees.
Such water-holes are focal points for forest animals; they
must come there to drink, despite the ever-present threat of
the tiger.

William Collins Sons and Co. Ltd
London · Glasgow · Sydney · Auckland
Toronto · Johannesburg

First published in Great Britain 1986
Copyright © Eddison/Sadd Editions Limited 1986

British Library Cataloguing in Publication Data
Thapar, Valmik
   Tiger : portrait of a predator
   1. Tigers   2. Wildlife refugees ——— India
   I. Title   II. Ziesler, Günter   III. Rathore,
Fateh Singh
   599.74′428   QL737.C23

ISBN 0-00-217449-9

AN EDDISON·SADD EDITION

Edited, designed and produced by
Eddison/Sadd Editions Limited
2 Kendall Place, London W1H 3AH

This book was produced in association
with Bruce Coleman Limited

Phototypeset by Bookworm Typesetting
Manchester, England
Origination by Columbia Offset, Singapore
Printed and bound by Tonsa, San Sebastian, Spain

सत्यमेव जयते

PRIME MINISTER

FOREWORD

Project Tiger was launched in 1973 out of concern for India's dwindling wilderness. While launching it, Shrimati Indira Gandhi described it as a token of "our newfound, but most welcome, concern for saving one of nature's most magnificent endowments for posterity".

The project has succeeded in putting this endangered species on a course of assured recovery. It has also helped to protect some of our finest forests and wilderness areas. It has inspired the establishment of more protected areas and the adoption of a National Wildlife Action Plan.

Shri Valmik Thapar has done well to tell the story of this experiment in wildlife conservation. He has particularly focussed on Ranthambhore, one of the more successful tiger reserves, whose story is told by Shri Fateh Singh Rathore. I hope that the book will help the public to understand the importance of conserving not only wildlife but our total environment.

The experience of Project Tiger will remain valuable for our efforts to meet the basic needs and requirements of our people without destroying the resource base.

New Delhi
November 1, 1985

CONTENTS

Camouflaged in the undergrowth, the large male Kublai
watches us intently. The tiger's vision is exceptional, by day
or by night, and will pick up the slightest movement in the
surrounding forest.

PREFACE

Ranthambhore is a very special haven for tigers, and in the following pages nearly a decade of work unfolds. Working with tigers is no easy task. Even today, locating tigers is difficult: studying them and photographing them is even more so. Several weeks can go by without as much as a glimpse of this elusive predator. Understanding the tiger is also an ongoing process and I think it unlikely that the process will ever come to an end. Final conclusions about tiger behaviour patterns and activities are difficult to make, as learning is a continuous process of observing and absorbing what one sees. This book is an attempt to provide glimpses and insights into the life of the world's most powerful and unpredictable predator. As long as people throughout the world are aware of the tiger and sensitive to its needs it has a chance of surviving into the future. I hope this book will help that awareness and understanding.

My special thanks go to Günter Ziesler for his superb photography and for bringing us all together; to Eddison/Sadd for their commitment to the idea; and to Fateh Singh for his knowledge, expertise and assistance in this complex task.

I must also take this opportunity to thank V.D. Sharma of the Rajasthan Wildlife Department, Romila, Raj, Tejbir, Angelika Hofer, the late Diana Wordsworth, Divya Chavda, Peter Lawton, Andrew Lowenthal, Goverdhan, Ghaffar, Badhya, Ramesh, Saed, Mahinder, Manohar, and all the staff at 'Project Tiger', Ranthambhore, for encouragement and help in so many ways.

Finally, my thanks go to those incredible tigers living today in the forests of Ranthambhore, without whose inspiration and involvement such a book would never have started.

VALMIK THAPAR
Ranthambhore 1985

One of the resident tigresses, Noon, rests at the edge of Rajbagh lake, lit by the setting sun. A typical scene in the forest of Ranthambhore.

CHAPTER ONE

A PREDATOR IN DECLINE

The image of the tiger today is one of power and mystery. But what of its past? The earliest evidence we have of the tiger in India, apart from fossil evidence, is that contained in the Harappan seals of the third millenium B.C. Many of these seals carry complex stylized images of the tiger, and their symbolism suggests a deep ritual significance. The ritual importance is carried over into later periods and is very evident in the Vedic texts of the first millenium B.C. in which the tiger, referred to as *Vyaghra*, symbolized power, strength and an aura of the unknown.

As the centuries rolled by, the tiger image seems to have flourished – appearing over and over again in carvings and artefacts, murals and mosaics, and the civic and religious records of many different cultures from North Africa and Mediterranean Europe in the west to China in the east. In the Indian subcontinent it pervaded every aspect of life and culture. The myths and legends of India have accorded a special place to nature, and especially to the tiger, and this most powerful of symbols has been adopted by a number of ruling families, including the Chola dynasty of A.D. 850-1014.

The Mughal, or Mogul, period in India, which lasted from 1526 to 1857, saw the introduction of *shikar* – the formal and highly organized form of hunting that was to last well into the present century. In its original form *shikar* did minimal damage. Weapons were restricted to bows and spears, and many of the Mughal emperors, such as Babar, Humayun, Akbar, Aurangzeb and Jehangir showed a remarkable sensitivity towards nature and the wildlife of the forests. Jehangir in particular was a born naturalist and kept detailed notes on the wildlife he encountered.

The real damage began during the eighteenth century, with the arrival of the Europeans. Their new technology and industrialization broke the traditional close links between man and nature in India. The British arrived with their superior firearms and quickly established themselves in the country. They were the rulers and conquerors; they had the leisure and power to hunt as and where they pleased – and their guns gave them a new and destructive supremacy over all animal life. The sport of shooting tigers became a symbol of prestige; the most exciting of all field sports. For the tiger it was the beginning of the end.

But the tiger as a symbol of power and mystery continued to exert a profound influence. Tipu Sultan, the ruler of Mysore state in the late eighteenth century, was a man obsessed with the tiger. Tipu really meant 'tiger', or 'king of the wilds', and he derived his name from a holy man. The concept of the tiger pervaded his whole being and Tipu Sultan claimed that he would rather live two days as a tiger than two hundred as a sheep. Everything he owned or possessed was adorned with the visual image of the tiger or its stripes, including his throne, his clothes, the uniforms of his soldiers, his handkerchiefs, his sword, his guns and their stocks, hammer and sights. His banner carried the legend, 'The tiger is God'.

Indian miniatures of the 16th and 17th centuries often
show the tiger in the Imperial Court as a symbol of power
and strength. This symbolism is deeply rooted in Indian
culture and dates back at least to 2500 B.C. – the date of the
pictorial seals discovered at Mohenjo-Daro in northwest Sind.

The Maharajas of India and the British together entered the nineteenth century in an orgy of hunting that threatened to destroy, for sport, a large part of India's natural fauna, especially the tiger. But amongst the thousands of hunters there were a few who recorded exciting and unusual encounters in the jungles of India.

One of the earliest descriptions of a tiger killing deer comes from Captain Thomas Williamson in his book *Oriental Field Sports* (1807). 'I crept close enough to get a good aim at a fine buck, which was not above a dozen yards from me. While I was levelling, I observed something strange agitate the grass, but a few feet on the other side of the buck. It was nothing less than the tail of the tiger, waving in that ecstatic manner we observe in cats about to seize a bird. The moment for drawing the trigger was delayed by the sight of what I did not at first sufficiently distinguish; and I should probably have fired at the deer, which I could scarcely miss, had not the tiger put in a more forcible claim by springing on the animal thus doubly devoted to destruction, and rendered it expedient for me to preserve the means of defence; not that I could with truth assert that I was so cool and collected at the moment to avail myself, had it been requisite, of the loaded piece I held in my hands.'

The intensity of the hunting obsession among British sportsmen is well stated even as early as 1833 by Captain A. Mundy in his book *Pen and Pencil Sketches, being the Journal of a Tour of India.* 'Thus in the space of about two hours, and within sight of the camp, we found and slew three tigers, a piece of good fortune rarely to be met with in these modern times, when the spread of cultivation and the zeal of the English sportsman have almost exterminated the breed of these animals.'

Some sportsmen recorded unique observations of interactions between animals. One such was William Rice who, in his book *Tiger Shooting in India* (1857) states, 'On still further following this tiger's tracks, we came upon a dead hunting cheetah (or hunting leopard) that had just been killed by the tiger, he having, no doubt, surprised the cheetah asleep, for the marks of the tiger's claws, from which blood still was flowing, were quite plain on the body.'

Official records for 1877 reveal that 819 persons and 16,137 cattle were killed by tigers and that 1,579 tigers were killed by man. I think it was at this point, towards the end of the nineteenth century, that tiger hunters felt their first pangs of guilt. The tiger was being decimated, and although this process was continually rationalized, odd remarks were creeping in about how tigers could no longer be found and killed in the numbers possible in the earlier

One day's 'bag'. An example of the carnage that took place in the 1930s when *shikar* was at the height of its popularity. In the course of my research, I reviewed the accounts of more than 10,000 successful tiger hunts over a 100-year period. The highest known individual score is the 1,100 tigers shot by the Maharaja of Surguja.

part of the century. Some sportsmen-naturalists were even far-sighted enough to suggest that certain natural habitats should be closed to sport while others remained open, so as to allow the tigers to recover.

The tiger had entered the twentieth century with its fate under a large question mark. Hunters basked in their glorious feats of tiger slaughter, and there was great competition to see which could better the other. Unfortunately the tiger was the victim of this competition. George Yule was a prolific hunter of the Victorian era and a member of the Bengal Civil Service. He stopped counting after his tally had reached 400 tigers. Gordon Cumming (1872) shot 73 tigers along the Narmada River, and ten tigers in five days on the Tapti River. William Rice shot 158 in Rajasthan in four years in the mid-nineteenth century. Colonel Nightingale shot more than 300 in the Hyderabad region. Montague Gerard accounted for 227 in central India and Hyderabad in 1903. Forsyth (1911) shot 39 tigers in eleven days. A hunt in 1919 yielded 120 tigers, 27 leopards and 15 sloth bears. General Wardrop (1921) shot seven adult tigers in seven days.

The records stretch on, but despite them there seemed for the first time to be a ray of hope on the horizon. People had started to take more interest in the natural history of the tiger and its behaviour. One such person was F.C. Hicks, a Deputy Conservator of the Imperial Forest Service. In his book *Forty Years Among the Wild Animals of India* (1910), he describes a unique encounter. 'During the beat the spotted head of a panther of extraordinary size pushed its way through the grass, followed by the unmistakable striped shoulders and body of a tiger, though looking a bit dirty, as if it had been rolling in ashes. I succeeded in dropping this extraordinary creature dead with a shot in the neck, and, on examining it, I found it to be a very old male hybrid, with both its teeth and claws much worn and broken. Its head and tail were purely that of a panther, but with a body, shoulders and neck ruff unmistakably that of a tiger.'

E.P. Stebbing in *The Diary of a Sportsman Naturalist in India* (1920), describes a night of observation. 'I was beginning to wonder whether the vigil was to be a blank when I suddenly saw two round beads of fire, twin stars set close together in the darkness of the forest on the other side of the clearing. I first thought of fire-flies, to dismiss the idea as quickly as it had flashed across my mind. An animal, and from their height probably a sambar, I surmised . . . I had not come out to kill so much as to watch, and I had not made up my mind as to whether I should fire or not when fate intervened, and one of the tragedies of the forest was enacted before my eyes. Almost without a sound a mighty black shadow, coming from our right rear, hurled itself through the air, and with a startled appealing bellow the lordly stag was borne to earth. A struggle of wildly kicking hoofs, a few gasps and gurgles . . . I drew a deep breath. The shape was a tiger and I wondered whether it had been stalking us when the sambar had so opportunely appeared on the scene or whether it was as unaware of our presence as we were of his.'

The more serious observers were now growing in numbers, and these were people prepared to give up the gun just to be able to look and learn. I think the first of these remarkable gentlemen was A.A. Dunbar Brander who spent 21 years in the Central Provinces as a member of the Forest Service. He says in his book *Wild Animals in Central India* (1923), 'During my service I kept diaries and notes of my doings and especially of anything of interest displayed by an animal. For about six years I practically ceased to shoot, and it is to this period that I am chiefly indebted; one can see so much more of an animal, and under such different circumstances, if one is not intent on killing it.'

The first real master of wildlife photography in India was F.W. Champion, whose books *With Camera in Tiger Land* (1927) and *The Jungle in Sunlight and Shadow* (1933) remain masterpieces in the art of nocturnal photography. Champion was also a forest officer who gave up the gun for the camera and started recording on film and through the written word his observations of the wild and its inhabitants. I think the tiger moved and affected him deeply, and he realized the extent of the senseless destruction that was taking place around him. He says in the introduction to *The Jungle in Sunlight and Shadow*, 'It has been written, also, in the hope that it may add a little to the accumulated knowledge of the intimate lives of some of the inhabitants of the jungle. And in the even greater hope that it may raise a deeper sympathy for wild creatures; that it may give some sportsmen cause to think twice before they pull the trigger on animals that, possibly, they often gain nothing by shooting; that it may remind others that life is the dearest possession of all the dwellers in the wild – a treasure of which they should not be deprived without very adequate reasons.'

His later years were devoted to watching and photographing the tiger. With single-minded dedication he worked for years using a trip-wire on cross-roads and paths in an effort to document the tiger and other nocturnal species on camera. In those days this was a complex operation. Champion could take only one picture a night, and his collection of pictures speaks volumes for the effort he must have put in.

Another exceptional man of these times was Jim Corbett, who worked on the railways. His relentless pursuits of man-eating tigers are famous, and even at the age of 63 he was still fit enough to roam the Indian jungles on foot. Unfortunately, Corbett's stories swept the length and breadth of the world and may have contributed to the feeling that all tigers were man-eaters and dangerous. This was not Corbett's intention but the sad result of his skilful writing. Some readers got so absorbed in the adventure of the pursuit that they gave little thought to Corbett's true feelings. In fact he loved the tiger, and his actions were governed by the highest moral principles.

Corbett had another rare expertise. He was master of the language of the jungle and had learnt it on foot. He had in his lifetime been able to attune himself to the 'jungle instinct' and the thinking of a tiger. He was the perfect tracker, and his book *Jungle Lore* (1953), will be a classic for decades to come. He was also greatly influenced by Champion's work in photography and was one of the first to document some of the tiger's natural behaviour using a movie camera. He even recorded a tiger killing naturally on film, and to the best of my knowledge is the only man ever to have secured film of a white tigress in the wild. Unfortunately, most of his footage was ruined by moisture, but still some 200 metres of film on tigers survives in the National Film Archive in London; a truly remarkable effort for the time.

Sadly, he and other concerned men were unable to prevent the massive destruction of the tiger that took place between 1930 and 1960. Between the British and the Indian ruling classes the records increased in leaps and bounds. Ranthambhore, the Maharaja of Jaipur's private hunting reserve, saw a peak of activity. In those days the 'shooting lodge' had spacious lawns where hunting parties played croquet and badminton, and took morning exercise on camel back for pleasure. Camps were laid out with large colourful tents called *shamianas* as the hunting parties awaited news of the tiger. The guests included His Majesty King George of Greece, the Duke of Gloucester, the Count and Countess Szechenyi, Princess Zia, the daughter of Tsar Nicholas the Second, the Georgian Prince Alec Mdvani, Earl Hopping, Sir Robert Throckmorton, Sir Beauchamp St. John, a series of Maharajas and a host of others.

Shooting records multiplied even faster than before. In the 1938/9 season, Lord Linlithgow, former Viceroy of India, shot 120 tigers in ten weeks in the Chitawan Valley of Nepal. The Maharaja of Udaipur shot at least 1,000 tigers, the Maharajkumar of Vijayanagaram over 325, the Maharaja of Surguja around 1,100, the Maharaja of Rewa 500, the Maharaja of Gauripur 500, and so on.

The move to independence gave a fresh lease of life to Indian hunters, who now went after the tiger with a vengeance. Even in the Forest Service, killing a tiger enhanced a man's status. It meant that he had understood the ways of the forest. Small and large *shikar* companies sprang up all over India, enticing sportsmen into what was described as the world's most exciting sport. The tiger population declined rapidly. It stood at around 40,000 at the turn of the century, and fell to about 4,000 in the fifties. The price of skins soared. The tiger appeared to be gasping for life. E.P. Gee, a noted naturalist of these times, writes in his book *The Wildlife of India* (1964), 'As I see it, there can be no doubt that at the present rate of cutting vegetation, overgrazing by domestic stock, and killing of wild animals in India, by the time public opinion can rally in support of wise conservation of wild life, there will be practically nothing left to conserve. There will be very little wild life left by the year A.D. 2000, only thirty-six years from now, except in zoological gardens.'

By the late sixties, many believed that the fate of the tiger was sealed. In 1969, when the Congress of IUCN (the International Union for Conservation of Nature and Natural Resources) was held in New Delhi, it was thought that the tiger population had fallen to 2,500. The Congress for the first time passed a resolution which resulted in the Indian tiger being added to the IUCN *Red Data Book*, which lists endangered species.

Indira Gandhi, then Prime Minister of India, felt strongly about protecting India's wilderness areas. In 1970 she spearheaded legislation banning tiger hunting and the export of skins. The tiger was getting a fresh lease of life; but would it be too late?

It was Guy Mountfort, an international conservationist who, at a joint meeting of IUCN and the World Wildlife Fund, proposed an international effort to create effective and fully equipped reserves for the long-term survival of the tiger. He also suggested that all efforts and resources be concentrated on the race of tigers that was still found in relatively large numbers, namely the Indian subspecies or royal Bengal tiger. The resources required were some £400,000 and the project was accepted and called 'Operation Tiger'.

In 1972 the Indian Government conducted their first ever census operation on the tiger. Nearly 5000 men were involved in this operation, and deep shock was expressed when the census estimated the population at only 1827 tigers.

In October of that same year H.R.H. Prince Bernhard of the Netherlands, President of the WWF, launched the appeal for funds. A special committee was created by Indira Gandhi to coordinate action in India under the chairmanship of Dr Karan Singh. The first five-year budget included £2.1 million expenditure by the Indian Government. Similar encouragement was received from the King of Nepal and the President of Bangladesh, and the neighbouring Himalayan state of Bhutan quickly added her support.

The subcontinent was at last taking positive action to protect the royal Bengal tiger. The WWF's international appeal raised more than £800,000 in 18 months. The original 'Tiger Task Force' of 1972 had selected nine areas to become special reserves, and in 1973 'Project Tiger' was inaugurated in Corbett National Park in Uttar Pradesh, under the directorship of Kailash Sankhala. By 1974 Ranthambhore had also been designated a 'Project Tiger' reserve.

All over the world, public awareness and sensitivity rallied to the cause of the tiger's conservation. Real animal furs lost their social importance as more and more people adopted the conservationist view. Fashions changed, and in many countries the wearing of skins from rare wild animals became more likely to attract anger and hostility than the envy and admiration of earlier years.

With the money that poured in to the WWF an infrastructure and a pool of equipment was created in the reserves. The Fund supplied forty vehicles, two launches for the Sundarbans mangrove swamps straddling the borders of India and Bangladesh, complete radio and wireless networks for several reserves, tractors, telemetry and capture equipment, and other research apparatus such as cameras, binoculars and night lenses. For the tiger, it was the first ray of hope.

In 1976, a mid-term appraisal conducted by the WWF revealed a dramatic improvement in the tiger's chances of survival. It was in that same year that Ranthambhore entered my life.

RANTHAMBHORE, FORTRESS HAVEN FOR WILDLIFE

How well I remember that day in early 1976. Life in Delhi had reached its lowest ebb as far as I was concerned. I just had to get away. Personal problems were crowding in on me, adding to the pressures of the city. I was cold and alone that winter, and I knew somehow that it was to be a period of much change for me. The time had come to leave my immediate environment and spend some time quietly contemplating my life, my needs and my future. I had heard a little about Ranthambhore, the unknown and unspoilt wildlife sanctuary 300 kilometres south of Delhi in Rajasthan Province, and I took a quick decision to go there, not knowing what the future might have in store. A few weeks spent among the wild forests and hills of the reserve would do wonders for my peace of mind. I already had a long-standing interest in natural history and I would enjoy discovering some of the forest animals and birds of Rajasthan. And who knows? With a great deal of luck I might even catch a glimpse of that most magnificent of India's wild animals, the tiger.

It was a strange six hours spent on the train, as it wound its way to Sawai Madhopur. While my eyes watched the flat dusty plains of Rajasthan, I thought of my past and the delight of leaving behind a superficial and vacuous existence. But my apprehensions began as I neared my destination. There was no sign of a forest: only the same dusty plains showing man's encroachment on nature and the devastation it creates.

Sawai Madhopur certainly provided no clue to what might lie ahead. Named after a former King of Jaipur, it was a typical district town, sprawling around the railway track which was obviously its only reason for existence. My heart sank a little, thinking of the endless train whistles which must surely frighten away any wildlife. As I stepped on to the platform I felt the piercing stares of people around me, all seeming to question my presence. The roles seemed reversed, with myself as the tourist attraction. I took the first horse-cart I could find and we jolted along to the Forest Department headquarters, through the dismal mess of concrete and brick structures that is the mark of every small town in India today. Smoke poured from the cement factory nearby, taking over the sky like a large grey cloud. My hopes of ever seeing a tiger sank.

I met Fateh Singh Rathore, the Field Director of the Park, at the barrack-like office of 'Project Tiger'. He looked a strange sight with his luxuriant moustaches and Stetson hat. Had I arrived in the American Wild West? I asked for permission to spend some time in the Park, and waited anxiously as he looked me up and down as if assessing whether or not the animals would approve. Fortunately I passed the test, and with great relief and a growing feeling of anticipation hired a jeep and driver and was on my way by the late afternoon.

Leaving the town, we followed a narrow metal road running parallel to a range of hills, and after several kilometres turned off onto a dirt track; but still there were few indications of what lay ahead, be it forest or wildlife. The road then turned sharply, and suddenly we were skimming along the rim of a deep ravine, bouncing and jolting over the stony track.

And then it came; the first thrill of excitement. Below a sheer rocky cliff

The idyllic setting of Jogi Mahal, nestling in the forest at the edge of Padam Talao. In the distance lies Rajbagh, the second of Ranthambhore's three lakes. Low hills surround the lakes, whose waters abound in fish, water snakes and soft-shelled turtles and support more than 100 Indian marsh crocodiles.

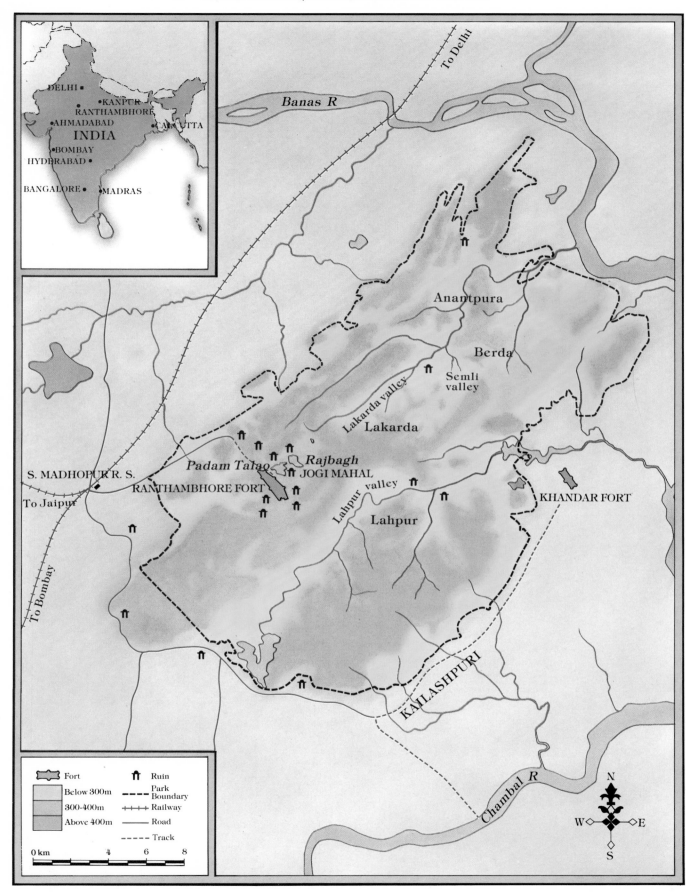

DELHI
KANPUR
RANTHAMBHORE
AHMADABAD
INDIA
BOMBAY
HYDERABAD
BANGALORE
MADRAS
CALCUTTA

Banas R

To Delhi

Anantpura

Berda

Lakarda valley

Semli valley

Lakarda

Padam Talao

Rajbagh

JOGI MAHAL

S. MADHOPUR R. S.

RANTHAMBHORE FORT

To Jaipur

Lahpur valley

Lahpur

KHANDAR FORT

To Bombay

KAILASHPURI

Chambal R

Fort

Below 300m

300-400m

Above 400m

Ruin

Park Boundary

Railway

Road

Track

0 km   4   6   8

N
W   E
S

LEFT Map 1. The main geographical and settlement features of the area around the Ranthambhore National Park in north-central India.

BELOW The enormous banyan tree just outside Jogi Mahal is one of the largest in India and must be several hundred years old. Its canopy shades a vast area providing welcome relief from the blistering sun and a permanent home for birds, snakes, bats, squirrels and a host of insect life.

stood an ancient but massive stone gate which must once have been flanked by fortress walls, long since crumbled. It was a royal entrance to Ranthambhore, constructed to protect the domain of kings and surviving today to protect a treasure of equal if not even greater value. Water flowed from the gate through a marble cow's head, forming a pool at the entrance. Beyond the gate the air cooled, the vegetation thickened and the sounds changed. The chatter of birds mixed incongruously with the groan of the jeep. Cresting a rise, we saw the incredible sight of the Ranthambhore fort, grey and looming, extending upwards from a steep cliff face. The sky was a clear blue; the forest around, a dull green. The huge walls glinted in the evening sunlight, looking for all the world as if man had decided to chisel a bit of nature, the upper fringe of the rock, rather than disturb or fight it.

We were close to our destination. I tried to look around me, straining to see through the trees for signs of life, but my eyes were not yet accustomed to seeing in the forest. It is a skill not easy to come by. I could see old peepal trees and large banyans and I wondered how much they had changed since the days of Ranthambhore's glory. We were now winding our way below the massive fort, and as we crossed the last rise the terrain changed dramatically. The steep hills gave way to a broad valley, dotted with low hills and large expanses of water, the largest clothed almost entirely in giant pink and white lotuses. It was the pink of innumerable folk paintings; a pink that I had never before believed possible. It was too much to assimilate all at once, this mix of history, man and nature.

As we branched off the road I thought we were plunging straight into the largest banyan tree I had ever seen. Two of its hundreds of roots formed a natural gateway to Jogi Mahal, the forest resthouse, which decades ago had been the residence of a temple priest. Before the driver could even stop I was rushing up the steps, across a wide terrace and through the high arched doorway. There at my feet lay the lake of lotuses I had glimpsed earlier, with the waters of the lake lapping peacefully against the base of the resthouse.

In the distance crocodiles lay sun-bathing; one with its jaw open, another swimming lazily in the water. Wild boar, chital and sambar were feeding on the lush grass growing on the banks of the lake. Some of the sambar were half immersed in the water, nibbling at the lotus leaves. Darters, herons, grebes and kingfishers flew around in abandon. Occasionally a large fish would slap the water. To the right of the lake were the remains of an old temple, and on one of the hills a guard post. Turning around, I looked back the way we had come. The vast banyan tree and the backdrop of the fort filled the horizon with their imposing presence. It was a hypnotic moment of great intensity, of indescribable beauty, and I suddenly felt exhausted. I knew then that Ranthambhore was going to mean something special to me.

The resthouse was simply appointed without the fuss or garishness of modern resthouses. There was no electricity, and Jogi Mahal was fortunately untouched by the onslaught of modernization. I wondered for how long this would hold true. Soon, the forest staff collected around; Laddu, the tiger tracker, Ramu, the wireless operator and Prahlad Singh, the driver. The chill of the night had descended and we lit a fire, the crackling of the firewood joining the nocturnal sounds of the forest. Crickets, nightjars, and owls had woken up to the dark. Small bats whizzed around and the large flying fox flapped above us. The conversation was exciting, with Laddu holding forth on the tiger and his activity in the dark of the night, and Ramu talking about the ghosts that were left behind when wars ravaged the area. Prahlad added that even today a few spears could be seen embedded in the fortress walls. It was my first introduction to life in the forest.

Without warning, this easy atmosphere was shattered by a loud booming noise lasting for nearly ten seconds. I took fright, and jumped, and amidst much laughter was told that this was the alarm call of the sambar. For them it was a normal night sound indicating the presence of a tiger or leopard. It would warn other deer that a predator was on the prowl and alert them to this danger. The call was repeated, echoing sharply off the fort walls. Torches were flashed around the thick roots of the banyan tree just in case there was something lurking around. Then a high-pitched shriek came from a little distance away. The chital, or spotted deer calling. The predator was moving. We were all on guard and I felt a shiver run down my spine as the tension mounted. After a while, the calls died away. The silence deepened and the forest relaxed again with the nocturnal sounds taking over. I felt part of that forest, even though only a small part. In Delhi one lives in isolation from nature and the forest suddenly puts you in your proper place. It had been a memorable evening. My eyes were heavy with sleep and I left the warmth of the fire to slink into my sleeping bag.

I woke with the sun and the startling early morning light, wondering about the night before and what the predator had found to eat. The banyan tree throbbed with life – peacocks, babblers, parakeets and mynahs were chattering away while a troop of langur monkeys jumped around in the branches. I hopped into the jeep and we took off. At the base of the fort was a small habitation, a tea shop and a few houses that belonged to the temple priest who managed the Ganesh temple up on the fort. Thousands of pilgrims walked up every week in search of spiritual elevation. My thoughts were suddenly brought to a halt by a man gesticulating wildly. He told us that during the night a leopard had chased a buffalo up the road we were on.

For me this was headline news, and we jumped off the jeep to verify the story. Sure enough the leopard's pug marks were clearly visible on the dirt track. We started to follow. The buffalo's marks were running ahead, but after a couple of hundred metres they stopped, then veered off the road as the fleeing animal sought safety. I saw a patch of blood, and then some buffalo hair. The grass had been flattened. This was where the leopard must have killed. Cautiously we followed a trail of blood and drag marks, and a hundred metres farther on lay the half-eaten carcass of a buffalo. It must have been an exhausting effort to drag it so far, but leopards prefer to eat in the thicker forest as it provides security. Laddu showed me the canine marks on the buffalo's neck, and how the leopard had split open the stomach – a characteristic feature of the leopard's eating habits.

The sambar is the only deer that ventures into the lakes to feed on the succulent water vegetation. Here a sambar hind rears onto her hind legs to lash out at another, while close by – quite unperturbed – an egret stands patiently on the back of a stag, waiting for a fish to stray within striking range.

We moved on around the first lake, Padam Talao. I saw the façade of the Ranthambhore fort, silently guarding its memories of the battles and wars which once raged around its ramparts. I wondered how this natural paradise had escaped the predatory instincts of man. Prahlad told me some of the history of the fort. It appears that no one seems to know exactly when Ranthambhore was built, but historians agree that it is one of India's oldest battlements. The aura that surrounds it is sad, giving a feel of the past, of valour, bravery and death. Today, overrun by vegetation, the forest is littered with the scattered remnants of small covered pavilions, or *chatris*, summer palaces, and crumbling guard posts — reminders of a historical past set in a wild present.

We moved on to the second lake, Rajbagh. In the middle of it stood an old lake palace with a road leading to the rear. There was the usual traditional courtyard with *chatris* and terraces at all four corners. I sat in one and looked out, savouring the sounds of birds as a cool breeze wafted up the lake. A large crocodile was basking in the sun, a group of wild boars were busy digging into the mud — a scene that has probably remained unchanged for hundreds of years.

Driving around this lake gave me my first opportunity to look at some of the wildlife at close quarters. The chital is small and sleek compared with the big and heavy sambar who has long ears, a doleful expression in his eyes, and a dark brown coat. The nilgai, or blue bull, is a large antelope, the male a kind of steel-grey colour in contrast to the pale fawn female. Another member of the antelope family is the Indian gazelle or cinkara; petite and elegant with large sensitive eyes. My peaceful reverie was suddenly shattered as Prahlad Singh screeched to a halt. He had spotted some tiger pug marks. I jumped out to examine them and there they were, clearly imprinted in the soil. With mounting anticipation we started following them on foot, but after a couple of kilometres they branched off into cover and disappeared. I was extremely disappointed but I was to learn later how evasive the tiger is and how difficult to sight.

Gradually I was being initiated into the ways of the forest, and the first ten days rolled by without my even knowing how or where they went. Waking to the sounds of birds we spent the days watching deer and antelope graze without a care in the world, looking at crocodiles basking in the sun, endlessly chasing the pug marks of leopard and tigers, and learning the

A family of langurs – the only primate in Ranthambhore – basking in the first warm rays of the morning sun. The monkeys are always alert, and bark loudly at any sign of a predator – an extremely useful guide to those searching the forests for leopards or tigers.

sign-language of the forest from vultures, peacocks and jackals. Dusk was a dramatic time, with animals congregating around water-holes, peacocks flying to their perches in the trees in constant fear of predation, crickets calling in the night, and the resounding alarms of deer signifying the movements of predators. And in the darkness we moved towards these sounds – looking, searching, peering, straining for that one encounter with a tiger or leopard. But in vain. Instead, other nocturnal animals would show themselves, like the jungle cat, civet cat and ratel, and the amazing porcupine with its quills upright in self-defence.

Exhausted and defeated by our failure to sight the tiger we would return and huddle around the fire, listening again to stories of other encounters, which only added to the acuteness of my frustration. I had only a few nights left to meet with the nocturnal 'king of the jungle'. My hope of seeing it was fast ebbing when late one evening a sharp sambar call startled me from my tea-drinking. Turning around I flashed my torch and about eight metres away, to my right, two green eyes were reflected back at me. My heart leaped, thinking it was a tiger. But no. It was a hyena loping past Jogi Mahal. No wonder the sambar had only called once, warning mothers to keep their young close to them. But it was a good sight; my first of a hyena. I felt that I was drawing closer to that invisible presence of the tiger and leopard which had so far evaded me.

I decided to make one last determined effort and set off with Prahlad and Laddu for a long night drive. Chilled to the bone, with torches flashing, we sped through the forest. As we came down an incline between two sharp cliffs we switched off the engine to listen to the sounds of the night. Suddenly the alarm call of the chital came, wild and shrill, shattering the night with its intensity. It called at least 40 times, its nearness confirming the proximity of a predator. Moving forward slowly, flashing a torch, I found two eyes glinting back at me. And there in all its splendour sat a leopard, feasting on a female chital. We sat silently. The leopard turned around and looked at us with disdain and then continued eating, unperturbed by our presence. It must have been over two metres in length, and its rosettes glowed in the torchlight. Quite suddenly it got up and walked by us before climbing up the branch of a banyan tree where it settled down, keeping a watchful eye on its kill.

I realized the rarity of what we had seen, and was mesmerized, sitting deathly still, not daring even to breathe as any movement might make the animal suspicious. But Prahlad was taking no risks, and drove off. Disturbing a predator at his meal is just not on. We were intruders, interrupting a critical moment in the leopard's day as stalking and killing are complex operations requiring immense skill and a great deal of physical effort. I felt in my bones that this was going to be a lucky night. I had already seen two predators, and was filled with a sense of expectation.

Soon after leaving the leopard I spotted a dark shape walking ahead of us on the forest road. Very slowly Prahlad closed the gap, the lights of the jeep glancing off roadside rocks and trees, repeatedly missing the animal as the track twisted and turned. But at last I saw it. The unmistakable glow of the striped coat; the powerful, unhurried, silent walk. It was my first tiger, confidently strolling down the middle of the road. The power and pure beauty of that moment, mixed with an aura of the unknown, cast a spell which was to become a driving passion in my life in the months ahead. We followed slowly and soon the tiger stepped aside to let us pass, watching us from three or four metres away, quite relaxed but intent.

To me it seemed to herald the beginning of a long relationship, and I hoped a fruitful one for both the tiger and me. This species has suffered sordid treatment at the hands of man. Wanton destruction for the sake of sport and skin had nearly sealed its fate. I wanted to do something. I had a lot to learn from Fateh Singh who had an uncanny rapport with the forest and its animals, the tiger in particular, and was a reservoir of knowledge and experience. He was to become my guide and mentor on many future visits to Ranthambhore. Gradually, in the course of many subsequent trips, I started to understand the habitat and history of the Park, delving deep into the

LEFT The roots of a banyan tree hold the ruins of an ancient palace gateway in an eerie, death-like embrace. Nature and history combine to create a unique atmosphere in the forest of Ranthambhore.

BELOW Nearly a thousand years old and several kilometres in circumference, the massive battlements of Ranthambhore enclose one of India's most ancient fortresses. Countless battles have raged around these walls, and even the great Mughal emperor Akbar laid siege to them. Today, leopards and tigers prowl the ruins.

ecology of the area, which was critical for any understanding of the tiger. Nine years have passed since my first trip, and I look back today in an attempt to understand these years, the forest and the changes.

Ranthambhore was once the hunting preserve of the erstwhile Maharajas of Jaipur. In 1957 it was declared a wildlife sanctuary and in 1974 it came under the protective umbrella of 'Project Tiger'. I think what saved Ranthambhore's ecological system was the fact that the Maharajas controlled the area rigorously and, fortunately, did not indulge in numerous tiger shoots. In 1981 it was awarded National Park status, and richly does it deserve this for it is undoubtedly amongst the finest natural areas of the world. It is a dry deciduous forest that sprawls across an area of 392 square kilometres. Nature overflows here with her bounty and variety. The area has a preponderance of dhok trees but there is an abundance of ancient banyan and peepal trees with their spreading roots adding to the general luxuriance of the area. Dotted all over are concentrations of mango trees, and evergreen belts criss-cross the forest with their thick growths of jamun. Here the water supply is constant and the temperatures cool even during the hottest months. Every now and again one stumbles upon massive rock formations, steep scarps, perennial lakes and streams. The forest also suddenly opens up into large areas of wild grass savanna. For an area of less than 400 square kilometres Ranthambhore has a remarkably rich and diverse flora and fauna. The species lists for the area include nearly 300 trees, 50 aquatic plants and more than 100 species of herbs, grasses, climbers and seasonal plants. The bird list for the National Park contains 272 species; the mammal list has 22. There are at least a dozen species of reptiles and amphibians, perhaps a dozen of fishes, and a profusion of insect life that has still to be catalogued.

With the passage of each season the forest changes colour. During the monsoon everything turns a vibrant and lush green, and the prevailing sound is that of gushing streams and waterfalls. At the onset of summer the contrast is sharp and the forest seems to shrivel under the scorching sun.

The wide grasslands burn with the heat, the rocks reflect back at you, and you feel the forest is melting. The forest clothes itself in ochre. The climate is subtropical, with extreme variations in temperature from 0° Centigrade in January to 48° Centigrade in June.

As the seasons change, so too do the behaviour patterns, movements and concentrations of the forest animals. The heat sends crocodiles into the water and the deer gather in large numbers around the remaining water-holes. Whether it be predator-prey relationships, or courtship, the weather cycles affect all aspects of life, clearly illustrating the continuous interdependence between the living organism and its environment.

The geology of the reserve is dominated by the Aravalli and Vindhyan mountain ranges, and the rock is mostly limestone, sandstone and shale.

LEFT When the rains begin in July, the forest bursts into a profusion of green growth. Torrents of water cascade down the hillsides bringing welcome relief from the heat and replenishing the water-holes for another year. For two months the rain pours down, the forest thickens, visibility is almost nil and the forest roads and tracks are washed away: access is almost impossible.

ABOVE Ranthambhore in April. The ground is hard and dry and most of the smaller water-holes and *nallahs* have already dried up. Yet ironically it is just at this time of year that parts of the forest erupt into vibrant colour as the 'flame of the forest' trees come into bloom.

Two hundred kilometres of jeepable, fair-weather roads provide excellent access to remote areas but, to the credit of the Park management, several 'sanctuaries' have been left untouched and isolated with no roads or human intrusion. This allows the animals the peace and privacy so necessary to their well-being and procreation. In Ranthambhore the primary aim of the management has been to leave nature to tend its own wards. Most of the personnel perform watchdog functions to ensure that poaching, illegal grazing, wood-cutting and other such human interference is prevented. Others traverse the forest on pre-determined routes to report on animal behaviour and concentrations, road conditions and tiger movements.

A complexity of problems faced the forest staff during my first year in Ranthambhore. The newly-designated 'Project Tiger' reserve contained sixteen villages, one thousand people and ten thousand cattle, and there is inherent in this situation a conflict between the protection of our wilds and protection of the human habitations within them. Effective conservation is possible only where human intrusions are minimal, otherwise the entire ecological balance is disturbed. Consequently the primary goal of 'Project Tiger' was the translocation of these villages to areas outside the Park.

The impact of human settlements in the forest takes several forms. Large herds of cattle that graze all day on the rolling grasslands strip the area of its grass. This deprives the deer and antelope of their food, and in turn affects the tiger who depends on these animals for survival. Wood, which is necessary for village fires and for building, is taken from the jungle causing further denudation and disturbance to game. The crops that are grown around these villages attract wild animals, and man then takes the law into his own hands, with disastrous consequences for the animals. Cattle that wander into the forest often fall easy prey to the tiger, and since man depends on his cattle for milk he will soon find a way of killing the tiger. This is sometimes done by poisoning the half-eaten carcass of the animal so that if the tiger returns to eat, he will also die. Domestic cattle can also transmit fatal diseases to wild animals which, having no natural immunity, may die in huge numbers. The problems were many but they had to be solved.

India is a large developing country of some 730 million people. Large populations are poor and it is a difficult process to persuade people to leave their traditional homes so that an undisturbed ecological system can exist. Somehow a balance must be struck so that both man and animal can live in

RIGHT Sixteen villages and more than 1,000 people were relocated in order to give Ranthambhore's tigers their chance. Today, a female nilgai wanders unhurriedly through the ruins of a village fast being reclaimed by nature. A decade ago not an animal would be seen within several kilometres of a forest village.

BELOW The beauty of the 'flame of the forest' is short-lived, but while the trees are in bloom their massed red flowers delight the eye and provide a welcome addition to the langurs' diet.

peace without intruding on or disturbing each other's territories. When I first went to Ranthambhore in 1976/7, Fateh Singh was in the process of shifting all the villages outside the boundaries of the Park. The programme met with immense resistance from the villagers, many of whose families had lived in the forest for over 200 years. It not only required hard work from the forest staff but also much understanding, tact and persuasion.

A variety of compensations were offered. The landless and the landed would all get an extra five *bighas* of land (about one-and-a-quarter hectares) in addition to what they originally owned. House sites and wells would be generously compensated for, and the resettlement would take place on agricultural land. The proposed new village would have a temple, a school and playground facilities normally out of the villagers' reach. Even so, the process was an uphill task as no incentive is enough when you are being uprooted from your traditional home.

Some of the villages did agree to move, and I remember those emotionally charged departures which left tears in the eyes of all. A particularly vivid incident occurred in April 1977. It was early evening and all the district officials had assembled in the village of Lahpur to pay compensation to the villagers. The money had arrived and was ready for distribution. Suddenly I heard loud voices. The villagers had decided to refuse the money and not move out. Fateh took control of the situation. Huddled together around a fire, he and a group of angry and emotional villagers spent the next three hours in heated discussion while accusations were hurled back and forth. I listened spellbound. Every detail of the villagers' lives, their perceptions and sensitivities, their children and wives and their future were discussed. I thought it was going to be hopeless, but Fateh's patience and tact won through. It was nearly midnight when the villagers agreed to accept the compensation and to move out, but only after their crops had been harvested. Their decision was tinged with a sadness and reluctance as this would be a radical change in the course of their lives. No longer would they live as a close community depending on each other for their daily needs. They would be a part of the mainstream, with all the benefits of modern civilization.

Now, seven years later, all the villagers have moved out of the Park. The last one moved voluntarily five years ago. One of the resettlement complexes is Kailashpuri, and there the majority of the people are happy with their new existence. Their village is now one of the most prosperous in the district.

Only a small number of people miss their traditional homes and sometimes, on special occasions, they will return to the now-deserted villages to perform religious ceremonies. In this way they keep their roots intact. Only time will tell whether their sacrifice has been worthwhile.

Painful though it has been, I know that this shifting of villages has been a vital factor in restoring a healthy and harmonious ecological balance to the forest. The abandoned village sites provide a vivid example of nature's regenerating powers. Grasses and shrubs have overrun old fields, and mosses and lichens have carpeted the stone walls of abandoned dwellings. Some of the sites, such as Anantpura, Berda and Lakarda, are now amongst the most likely spots in which to find tigers, leopards and bears. Deer and antelope have occupied the area as well and only a practised eye would be able to make out that there was a human habitation here only a decade ago.

Today, the forest throbs with activity, and with an abundance of plant and animal life. Large populations of sambar, who prefer to eat shoots growing in the water of the lake, rarely compete with the chital who prefer the grasses that grow on land. The langur monkeys have an abundance of wild fruit trees, and their stomachs are specially chambered to allow them to digest the leaves. The blue bull is seen grazing away from the lake areas and the delicate cinkaras, who obtain water from the plants they eat, frequent the remote hard-ground plateau and the hills of the interior. Sloth bears thrive on wild fruits and wild boars dig up the ground in search of roots.

The dark brings out hares, porcupines, jungle cats, civets, ratels, hyenas and leopards. The tiger, too, is now numerous; but even more significant are the changes that have taken place in the behaviour of this remarkable animal. Ranthambhore has evolved. But how? And why?

In 1976 Ranthambhore was an exceedingly quiet place and relatively unknown. Months could pass between visitors, and tiger sightings were few and far between. Weeks might go by with no more than a brief nocturnal glimpse of the tiger before it disappeared into the thicker security of the forest. The tiger was elusive and shy of humans: getting close enough to study and understand it seemed an almost impossible goal. Those were days of inordinate patience, of endless games of watching and waiting. Fresh pug marks were a cause for much jubilation: a tiger sighting called for a major celebration. Between 1976 and 1979 I never once had a glimpse of a tiger drinking or submerged in water, strolling at the edge of the lake or sitting out in an open area. The tiger kept to the dense forest, out of sight.

By the time 1980 arrived, a profound change was taking place; a change I could feel in my very bones. Not only were pug marks found on most of the dirt tracks, but tiger sightings had increased tenfold. It was at this point that I discovered that my earlier judgments on tiger behaviour would have to be revised. It suddenly seemed that the years before were like a preliminary report on tiger activity. I had made many errors in my understanding; made many quick generalizations. Now I was discarding some traditionally held theories on tiger behaviour.

But exactly what was happening? The tiger population had certainly increased, but I had now to think of *why* the tiger was more relaxed and confident, fearless of the human presence. There seemed a steady and continuous increase in tiger activity throughout this dry, deciduous habitat and especially in the more open areas and on the edges of the lakes. Tigers had started appearing from everywhere, and their increased activity was not only nocturnal but equally diurnal. On one occasion I spotted a tigress stalking the edge of a lake in mid-afternoon, when the temperature was 45° Centigrade. She was carefully watching a group of sambar, grazing – almost immersed – in the still waters of the lake. Suddenly, and much to my surprise, she took off at great speed into the water, first wading and then swimming in relentless pursuit of the startled deer who rapidly fled to the far corners of the lake. The tigress then proceeded to sit in the middle of the lake, completely relaxed and at ease – astonishing behaviour for a formerly nocturnal hunter. I also remember once sitting on the terrace of Jogi Mahal sipping a cup of coffee and watching a herd of spotted deer grazing at the edge of the lake when suddenly a tiger bounded out, killed a doe and rushed back into the tall grass with her. I was stunned by what I had seen. These incidents, and others, proved beyond doubt that the tiger was discarding its nocturnal cloak – a development that gave me new and startling insights into the thinking mind of the tiger. I have tried later on in the book to explain some of these developments.

In the last ten years the Ranthambhore population of the tiger has increased from 14 to 40, just under three times the original figure, and this is definitely a contributing reason for the increase in tiger sightings. But why in broad daylight? I think that in the mid-seventies, when 'Project Tiger' started and the ban on tiger shooting was relatively recent, the tiger retained the nocturnal cloak that had protected it for over a century. Many tigresses must have heard the sound of a gun, experienced predation by man, and because of this their cubs must have been taught to shy away from man so as to protect themselves. To do so would mean a totally nocturnal existence, moving out only under the blanket of darkness. Up to 1979 Ranthambhore still contained villages, and this was yet another factor which must have contributed to the tigers' fear of man.

But from 1979 onwards there was no human encroachment. New generations of tigers were being born to mothers who had never known man's aggression. The mother was no longer teaching them to avoid man since there were none to avoid except for the occasional jeep-load of curious observers. The tigers were once again coming into their own. They were using both day and night to hunt, and were following the seasonal movements and behaviour of the deer and antelope. It was no longer necessary for them to stick to the dense areas of the forest; they were quite confident walking on roads, open grasslands and even around Jogi Mahal. The tigers' whole perception had changed – they were now the fearless kings of the jungle and man, the respectful observer, had been removed from his dastardly role as predator. But it had taken ten years of complete protection in Ranthambhore for the fear to be removed.

Early morning sun highlights the towering walls of Ranthambhore fortress and the forest resthouse of Jogi Mahal. Sambar are quietly grazing the lush green vegetation in Padam Talao as Kublai, one of Ranthambhore's magnificent male tigers, walks past.

CHAPTER THREE

THE LANGUAGE OF THE FOREST

It is 6.15 a.m. on 26 December 1982, and my eyes blink open. It is strange how the sleep cycle adjusts to the forest and the moment of dawn. It is a cold and wintry morning, and first light has already lit the far horizon. The temperature is 3° Centigrade. The forest is silent except for the early sounds of parakeets and partridges as they greet the new day. Warmly clad, we get ready to search for the tiger. Last-minute checks are made of cameras, films, binoculars and notebooks as we quickly pile into the jeep.

In this search-and-find operation, mobility is primarily confined to the use of open jeeps, which traverse the few hundred kilometres of roads that exist within the forest. Walking, unless it serves a specific purpose like tracking a particular tiger, is a disturbance not only for the tiger but for all the other animals as well, who rapidly move off and become unnaturally suspicious. The jeep is an object that the wild inhabitants of the forest have gradually come to accept, and only from a jeep is it possible to observe tigers and other animals for long periods at a time. The jeep is a noisy vehicle, and to be most effective it should be used as a listening post. You move a short distance, and then stop in order to listen to the sounds of the forest.

By 6.25 a.m. we are off. The icy wind numbs our faces and I am thankful for the warm gloves protecting my hands as a light frost has formed overnight. We stop at a point between the two lakes (Stop 1 on Map 2, p.34) – a marvellous vantage point from where, in the early morning, the Ranthambhore fort looms larger than ever, filling the horizon. The glow of the sun bounces off the walls, bathing the ramparts in a golden hue.

We look down at the ground, and our examination reveals that a tigress has moved here quite recently. Her pug marks are fresh and seem to be leading towards Rajbagh. It appears that she is of medium size as her pug mark is not too large, and the slightly tapering pad gives us a clear indication of her sex. Our excitement mounts as we follow the pug marks and cross to the area of the second lake. In the distance a herd of chital are grazing. To our right two sambar stags are sparring. This is their rutting period and the forest reverberates with the sounds of clashing antlers. Unfortunately our excitement is short-lived. After a few hundred metres the pug marks veer off into the forest and it soon becomes impossible to follow them in the jeep.

We drive a short distance and pause (Stop 2) to let our ears take over. After a few minutes the silence is shattered by the continuous high-pitched shrieks of an animal, interspersed with the loud booming call of another. There is a surge of excitement and tension in the jeep. The chital and sambar are now shrieking with rapid intensity. Within a few minutes nearly 75 alarm calls have echoed off the hills. The regularity of the calls is a definite indication that the deer are actually seeing the tiger. The calls are rolling off the upper slopes of a nearby hill, but the lie of the land blocks any possibility of access for the jeep and we are forced to sit and listen, our frustration rising with the crescendo of sound.

As the sun rises over Rajbagh its warming rays begin to disperse the morning mist. It is a critical time of day for us as we watch and listen for the sound of alarm calls, for at this time of day the tiger is abroad, patrolling his territory and choosing the shady spot in which he will rest in the heat of the day.

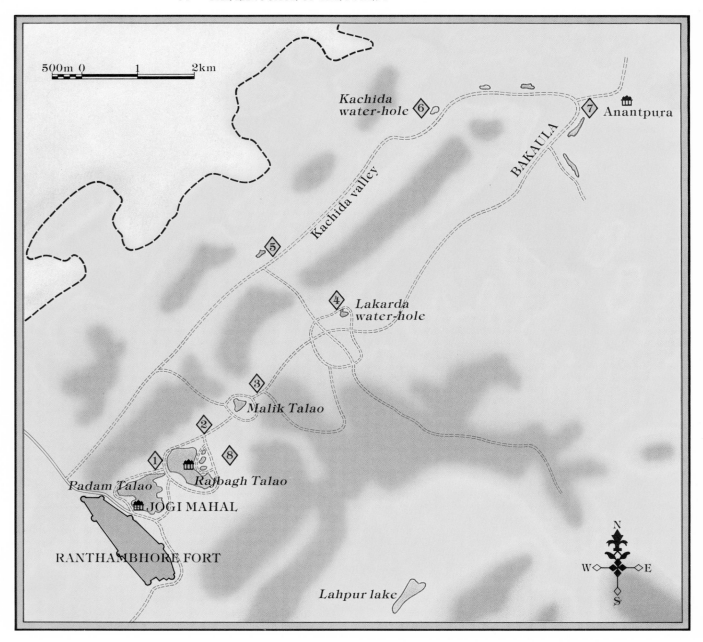

ABOVE Map 2. The route taken on our drive through the forests of Ranthambhore, showing the locations at which various observations were made (see text).

Soon the calls die away. The tiger has moved off, probably into a deep *nallah* or stream, to rest for the day. We are so close to the tiger, yet so far. But it is these alarm calls that we have to tune in to. The chital is nervous and edgy, and will call in alarm even when only slightly suspicious. Its call therefore does not always indicate danger, and on several occasions we have been misled and sent on a wild goose chase. The sambar, on the other hand, is the largest Indian deer and exceedingly confident. It seldom calls without good reason and is an excellent indicator of the presence of a tiger.

The time is now 7.30 a.m. The cacophony of sound that signified the movement of a predator has died away but it has left behind in the jeep an eerie tension and an electric atmosphere. We move on. All the deer and antelope in an area of several square kilometres have been warned that a tiger is around. Suddenly I spot three sambar stags. They are standing in the lake with their noses stretched out, sniffing the air. Their tails are raised and their forefeet are stamping nervously. The forest is silent, with no sounds of alarm, but the sambar are clearly giving off warning signs and I conclude that they must have picked up the smell of a fresh tiger spray-mark. Slowly they relax again; the moment of alarm has passed. We drive round the third lake, Malik Talao, and arrive at one of the main cross-roads of the forest (Stop 3). At this point two *nallahs* and two roads meet at a junction. The tiger is a soft-padded animal and enjoys walking on man-made roads, animal paths and along dried-up stream beds. The night before we had swept this area clean of all animal imprints so that now, with luck, we should be able to unravel the story of the night's activities.

As we get off the jeep our excitement soars. Before us lies an incredible record of events. From the freshness of the imprints it appears that the first to walk past was a sloth bear, leaving his distinctive, near-human footprints. A large male tiger had crossed later making a squarer impression. Then a young leopard followed by two jungle cats had walked across the junction and into a dry stream bed beyond. Chital and sambar had also crossed. And three porcupines. But the freshest marks of all are those of a tigress with two, or possibly more, cubs. The pug marks are imprinted in the soil with superb clarity and not even the edges have been disturbed either by the breeze or by the passage of another animal or bird. Even more exciting is the single thick line running across the junction with the pug marks of the tigress. Our hearts leap into our mouths. It is a drag mark. And with the line are some drops of blood. The tigress had killed a deer nearby and, followed by her cubs, had dragged the carcass across the junction, pulling it by the neck with the hind legs of the animal dragging against the earth. Finding such a drag mark is a rare stroke of luck, and we now begin a careful pursuit with a feeling of anticipation. Finding a tiger with a kill is unusual enough, but to find a tigress and cubs with a kill is the dream of a naturalist. The drag marks lead us towards the thicker areas of the forest and we follow in the jeep, bumping over the grass, rocks and dips until we can go no farther. Then we switch off the engine and sit in total silence. The tigress is aggressive and ruthless when with cubs and a kill, and great caution is required in this search operation.

BELOW Tails up, feet stamping, three nervous sambar stags scan the shores of the lake for signs of danger. This time it was a false alarm; the deer had caught the scent of a tiger drifting on the air – perhaps from a recent spray-mark in the lakeside grass. This is the language of the forest; the sights and sounds that must be understood if one is ever to see the leopard or the tiger.

RIGHT A rare sight. A large male tiger has walked along the forest road, placing his hind feet precisely in the imprints left by the forefeet, so leaving a single line of prints. Fresh prints, examined in the early morning before wind or other animals have disturbed them, can reveal the sex and general size of the animal as well as its activities and movements. The pug marks of the male are larger, broader and squarer than those of the female.

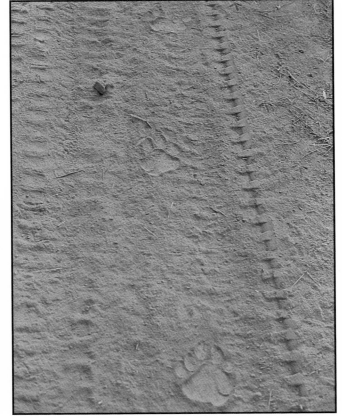

ABOVE Deciphering and following animal tracks is an exciting exercise in detective work and one that invariably has the adrenalin flowing in anticipation of a sighting. Here a tigress, revealed by the tapering shape of her pad, has shared a forest track with a sloth bear. Her tracks are the fresher of the two, indicating that she probably passed this way an hour or two after the bear.

RIGHT A fresh drag mark is the dream of every forest naturalist. Here the author examines a broad drag mark spotted with drops of blood and animal hairs, where a tigress has dragged the carcass of a large sambar towards thicker cover in order to feed. When the prey is small the tiger will carry it by the neck and the animal's trailing hind legs leave a narrow scrape in the ground. If the prey is large and heavy, the tiger walks backwards, dragging the carcass along the ground leaving a broad drag mark.

A hundred metres or so away we suddenly hear that delightful early-morning sound of crows cawing, a sound which normally indicates the presence of meat. In this case the sound is pinpointing the exact position of the tigress. Our eyes scan desperately. Way out in the distance we see two crows flying around a tree. The tigress and cubs must surely be there. But our hearts sink as we realize the area is so thick and inaccessible that there is no way through for the jeep. The tigress has chosen her spot well. We sit back in frustration. Then the call of the peacock resounds from the same location and we see a male bird burst into flight in alarm. These birds provide another excellent indication of the position of a tiger. They feed all day long in the forest in their thousands and act like sentries to the forest community. When deer are absent, it is important to pursue the alarms of peacocks and often I have discovered tigers through them. However, their reactions must be assessed carefully as they also call in alarm for birds of prey, jungle cats, jackals and leopards.

We sit listening to the forest. A woodpecker flashes by me, the deep gold of his back catching the sun as he lands heavily on a tree trunk and starts his tapping on the bark, looking eagerly for insects. In the distance a flock of green pigeons lands on a tree to bask in the warmth. Parakeets shriek loudly as they fly from tree to tree. Some metres from us four partridges are sunning themselves. The moment is splendid, but of the tigress there is no sight. The forest acts as a wall around her.

Sick with frustration we leave the area. The time is now 8.30 a.m. The sun is quite bright. We climb a hill and drive along a ridge, our eyes scanning to right and left, constantly adjusting to light and shade in a continuous effort to penetrate the forest, to glimpse any movement, shadow or shape that is not familiar in the lie of the land. After years of roaming the forest even a rock out of place is subconsciously recorded by the eye. Our ears strain to hear alarm calls, even above the noise of the jeep. Our eyes look for stripes in every bush and patch of grass, sweeping back and forth across the nooks, crevices, dips, hollows, grass banks, stream beds and thick bushes that tigers use to rest in, or position themselves on, in anticipation of a kill. In Ranthambhore the jeepable roads have been planned well, winding around the terrain in tandem with the movement patterns of tigers. And because of this the tigers use the roads regularly. They have definite and individually distinctive patterns of movement and we have become familiar with the movements of no fewer than 14 tigers in different parts of the forest.

As we approach the Lakarda water-hole (Stop 4) a strong musky odour brings the jeep to a grinding halt. It is the fresh scent of a tiger, left behind on a bush. This is where the human nose starts to complement the other senses. A strong odour is an indication of the recent presence of a tiger. As the animal roams it sprays various trees in its range in order to assert its territorial claims. Getting down from the jeep we let the smell of the tiger invade our senses, and then examine the area around the water-hole. A tiger has recently quenched his thirst and then walked off into a large deep ravine. A sloth bear has also passed this way. We sit listening to the sounds of parakeets, bulbuls, mynahs and a couple of chirpy tree-pies – small scavenging birds whose activities are another important indication when looking for tigers.

On a tree near the water-hole sits a crested serpent eagle, his talons clenched over a small snake which he is attempting to eat. Nearby a small blue kingfisher sits in anticipation of a fish. But my thoughts of kingfishers as master fishermen are rudely interrupted by the alarm call of a chital. Alert, we listen for some regularity in the call. It barks out six times. We move off a few hundred metres towards the Lakarda meadow and my eyes spot a chital doe stamping her foot, her tail raised, looking straight towards a patch of long grass. She calls ten times and then another doe behind her takes up the shrieking. I think to myself that it just has to be for a tiger. The regularity and intensity of the chital's alarm are so convincing. My eyes search for stripes in the grass but I can see nothing. We move in closer; I am expecting a tiger's face to pop out. The excitement mounts. There is a movement in the grass. And out comes a jungle cat whose fawn coat glistens in the sun as she

OVERLEAF The jungle cat is one of the rarest and most elusive of Ranthambhore's predators. It feeds mainly on birds, mice and hares, but despite its small size its characteristic feline movements through the grass can cause alarm even among herds of chital.

disappears behind a bush. I am amazed. Chital behaving with all the frantic alarm of a tiger scare! And just when I was certain about the presence of a tiger. The jungle is always full of surprises.

It is 9.15 a.m. by now and we move on towards the Kachida valley (Stop 5). The road winds up a hill, passing by some impressive rock formations before descending into a thick, shady valley where the temperature is always a few degrees cooler. After driving a few kilometres we find that there are no traces at all of pug marks. Looking skywards my eyes spot a group of circling vultures. We stop, and binoculars come out to investigate. Six white-backed vultures are circling the base of a cliff, while four more sit on a nearby tree. On yet another tree some crows are flitting around. Suddenly the low-pitched grunt of the nilgai or blue bull echoes off the cliff. It calls six times. Everything points to another tiger with a kill. The blue bull has an

Hectic activity among tree-pies, jungle crows and vultures is often a good indication of a nearby tiger kill, and a group of vultures sitting patiently in a tree, scanning the ground below, will always bring our jeep to an immediate halt with a thrill of anticipation. The vultures are in no hurry. They will sit for hours – days if necessary – waiting their chance to scavenge on the carcass as soon as the tiger moves away.

unusual call and many an experienced naturalist has mistaken the sound for that of a tiger. Though the animal only calls a few times on sighting a predator, the sound is sufficient to confirm the presence of one. Almost immediately, the sound is followed by the high-pitched wail of jackals. They have smelled the meat and sensed the tiger. The call is a special sound the jackal makes when a tiger is nearby. Once again we are within one kilometre of a kill – with no way of getting to it.

We watch the vultures for a while. These scavenging birds have sharp eyesight and can spot a carcass from high above. Then they circle or sit on a nearby tree, especially when a tiger is present. Only when the tiger has left can they land and gorge themselves. But there are many examples of over-anxious and hungry vultures attempting to feed on a kill not realizing the nearness of the tiger. Bloated and unable to take off swiftly, they have ended up being charged, swatted and killed. I have found that an excellent indication of a kill is given by a solitary Egyptian vulture, or sometimes a pair. They will either circle the kill or sit quietly on a nearby tree, especially when a tiger is present, and being white birds they are easily visible. In Ranthambhore the tigers tend to protect their food zealously from vultures, crows, tree-pies and other scavengers, but I have also come to the conclusion that vulture activity is used by the tigers as an aid in locating carcasses – either of animals that have died naturally or of animals killed by other predators. On several occasions I have known male tigers appear from nowhere to steal the kill of a tigress. I have also seen tigers suddenly appear and chase feeding vultures from a carcass.

Our spirits have sagged considerably since the day's promising start, but we move on, and at 9.45 a.m. we arrive at the Kachida water-hole (Stop 6). The only interesting tracks are those of a striped hyena which has stopped to have a drink of water in the night. A leopard has also followed in its footsteps. There is nothing more to be learned so we move on, soon entering Bakaula – a thick and lush evergreen area which has a perpetual supply of water. It has some splendid landscapes and the whole area has a rather special kind of beauty. On one side sharp and dramatic cliffs rise up to meet the sky, on the other are gentle low-lying hills, and in between – as if holding the two apart – is an evergreen belt interspersed with pools of water and the quiet sound of its gurgling.

Suddenly on the road ahead we see a large lump of faeces, which looks like that of a tiger. We halt the jeep (Stop 7) to investigate, and on examination we find that the faeces contain chital hair. The lump is quite fresh, and with it are the pug marks of a large male tiger. He would have eaten maybe a day earlier. Samples of faeces are usually to be found in the middle of the road or at the edges and they provide interesting information. Their examination can reveal a variety of different contents from the hair of an animal eaten, to mud, grass, porcupine quills and peacock feathers, thus revealing the diversity of the tiger's diet.

We now have little chance of sighting a tiger so we begin our homeward journey. It is 10.30 a.m. The sun is high, the temperature warm. At this time of day tigers sleep in cool, shady areas. Exciting as the morning has been, we have been frustrated in all our efforts. Driving along we suddenly spot the trunk of a tree that has been raked repeatedly by tiger claws. Tigers regularly indulge in this activity to assert their rights over a particular spot. At the edge of the road the tiger has also scratched marks in the soil in typical feline fashion. High in the tree a spotted owlet peeps out of a hole.

We move on and away from Bakaula. A pair of Bonelli's eagles circles a cliff and we stop and watch them. We wait for nearly 20 minutes for sounds of alarm, but the forest is silent. Two stork-billed kingfishers chatter away from the branch of a jamun tree. A brown fishing owl peers out from a fork of another tree. The male tiger's pug marks have followed the road for nearly three kilometres before disappearing into a ravine. Three times this tiger has sat down in the middle of the road leaving the imprint of his body in the soft soil. The pug marks not only indicate the sex of the tiger, but also the general size of the animal. An estimate of size can also be made from the length of the stride. However, great care is needed for examining tracks. Tigers sometimes walk by placing the hind foot over the mark of the forefoot, thereby producing a single spoor.

As we head for home my thoughts dwell on the tiger and its evasive nature. We have tried desperately to see one and I am sure a few of them were quietly chuckling at our attempts from behind a bush, wondering why this human species should ever attempt to match its skills against a super-predator camouflaged by the jungle. But even without the tiger the drive has been worth it. We have found evidence of eight or nine tigers, two leopards, two bears, a hyena and many other smaller mammals. We have seen over a hundred deer and antelope and countless varieties of birds. We have seen the throbbing life that inhabits the forest system and makes it a world of its own.

Our thoughts go to planning our evening drive according to the morning's

ABOVE This spotted owlet, well protected in its deep nest-hole, is just one of several owl species that live in Ranthambhore and prey on small mammals and reptiles.

LEFT Tigers and tigresses alike will repeatedly leave their claw marks high on the trunks and branches of particular trees in their territory. In the past this was thought to be the tiger's way of sharpening its claws and of cleaning them of shreds of rotten meat or other debris. Today it is seen more as a territorial declaration. The marks give a clear indication of the animal's size; this tiger has raked the tree some 3m above the ground.

ABOVE Greylag geese are winter visitors to Ranthambhore, arriving at the end of November and leaving again late in March. They spend most of the day resting around the lakes, but in the evenings they take off in large flocks to feed in the grain fields of villages outside the Park.

evidence. At the edge of Rajbagh a gaggle of greylag geese is basking in the sun. The birds spend the nights in surrounding fields and the days around Ranthambhore's lakes. Around them, busily fishing, are nearly a dozen painted storks. We pass the deserted ruins of the lake palace just before Jogi Mahal. We are pleasantly tired, relaxed, discussing the evening's activities. And in that unguarded moment – almost on our own doorstep – the forest springs its surprise. A shadow lurks in the *chatri* of the palace. Surely it is wishful thinking. But no. We screech to a halt. We move in closer and can hardly believe our eyes There it is; a tiger, fast asleep in the *chatri* (Stop 8).

Never before have we found a tiger in this palace. There is a flurry of activity – we can't believe our luck. It is the last place we would have thought of looking. Cameras are positioned, binoculars and notebooks activated. It is a tigress and we recognize her facial markings. She is Nick Ear, whom we have known for two months. She opens her eyes a few times in response to the sounds of the jeep but then continues to sleep in this incredible and historic setting. We watch her for nearly two hours. A couple of crocodiles bask at the edge of the lake below the *chatri*. The forest is quiet, her presence has not been revealed. I think of the past when kings and queens must have sat in this *chatri* and gazed across the lake, with music in the background. It is a place to which I have often come to sit and watch the activity on the lake. Today Nick Ear is haunting it with her presence. Times have changed. At 1.00 p.m. she disappears into the palace.

We decide to return for an hour to Jogi Mahal. Back to base we drive, exhilarated by this successful culmination of an amazing morning. As we get off the jeep we hear the sharp barking of the langur monkeys and see a troop sitting at the far side of the lake. They have spotted the tigress in the palace. It is easier for them than it is for us. With their excellent position high up in the trees they are super-efficient sentries. They scan the forest with their

RIGHT A parakeet peers from its nesthole in the trunk of an old tree. Ranthambhore has a large population of these birds, whose bright colours and shrill calls enliven the gloom of the forest canopy.

The unforgettable sight that greeted us at the end of our drive. Shaded by an ancient banyan tree, Nick Ear sprawls fast asleep in the an old *chatri* of the Rajbagh lake palace. A queen of the Ranthambhore forest had moved in to claim one of the ancient palaces of kings and emperors.

acute vision and their alarm call reverberates sharply through the forest at the presence of a predator. It will be a short stop at Jogi Mahal as we must soon return to Nick Ear and spend the evening with her.

It is fortunate that Jogi Mahal is in the heart of the forest. At the first sound of any alarm we can dash off to investigate. One must always be ready to move quickly, and 30 per cent of the time I have found success. When the forest explodes with the alarms of deer, monkey or peacock it is a moment of tension. At other times you may only hear a few calls but even then the pursuit of them is a must. I remember that one of my most memorable encounters in the forest took place after hearing just six alarm calls of the spotted deer. We responded, and our reward was five hours of observation of a leopardess, her two cubs and a hyena, all interacting over a chital kill.

Learning this language of the forest is very time-consuming. And each forest has a different language, dependent on the forest type, the lie of the land, the diversity and population dynamics of the inhabitants, the effect of efficient management techniques and the control of human pressure and disturbance by graziers, poachers and cattle. For instance, in Ranthambhore, because it is a dry deciduous forest, visibility is good. There is little human disturbance so the tiger is diurnal. But in other areas where forests are thicker and human disturbance greater, the tiger is nocturnal and the interpretation of the language is very different. Seldom do two forest systems show much similarity in the detail of their language. Instinct and experience must combine with vision and sound and it is through this synchronous working and flow that an understanding of a forest system grows. I have a great belief in instinct – especially when there are no indications on the ground and on many occasions I have found myself checking particular spots on instinct – and finding unusual tiger activity. At other times tigers are encountered quite by chance – walking along the road or sitting in the middle of it. I remember once while circling an area in the forest I suddenly came across several sets of very fresh marks. I got down to examine them more closely, following them along the track until they disappeared into some thick undergrowth. I lifted my eyes from the ground to find a large male tiger looking at me curiously from behind a thick bush less than two metres away. Startled, I backed away slowly, hardly daring to breathe. I was fortunate that day. The tiger was not in an aggressive mood and remained perfectly at ease with my presence as I sat and watched him for the next five hours.

In years past, tiger activity went through a fairly predictable daily cycle. The early morning might provide indications of a kill or signs of a tiger moving for shelter from the sun, basking for a few minutes in the first rays. In the late afternoon a tiger might move to quench his thirst or take position in anticipation of a kill. Dawn and dusk would bring about an intensity in tiger activity and alarm calls would reach a peak. But in recent years we have been forced to be on the alert all through the day due to the tiger's change to completely diurnal behaviour. Many an exciting conversation at Jogi Mahal has been rudely interrupted by me dashing off in a jeep, leaving the others wondering what had happened! But investigations of alarms and scares must be handled with great caution so as not to disturb a lurking predator. There are many nuances within the language, and they must be learned. But you can never know enough. You can only absorb what each new day brings, and this process of absorption is infinite; it has no beginning, no end. The more you think you know, the more you realize how little you know. But, however imperfect, it is the understanding of this forest language that makes it possible to obtain glimpses into the life of the tiger.

CHAPTER FOUR

THE LIFE OF THE TIGER

Observing tigers in the wild must surely be one of the most time-consuming activities in the entire field of natural history. It requires infinite patience and perseverance – not only when the tiger is nowhere to be found but even when he is right there in front of you. And the reason is very simple. Like most hunters, and especially the larger ones, the tiger spends most of its 24-hour cycle resting; always watchful, ever alert, but conserving its energy. Even after watching a tiger for six hours without a break you would count yourself lucky to see 60 seconds of exciting action.

For 80 per cent of its time the tiger sits or sleeps; dozing in a shady, strategically-placed spot during the day, occasionally getting up to stretch or to watch a herd of deer passing in the distance. Early morning and late evening are times for grooming, when the tiger will spend long periods licking the fur of its paws, chest and back. On a hot day these too would be the times to stroll to a stream or water-hole for a refreshing drink or a soak.

For perhaps ten per cent of the time I have encountered tigers walking for long distances along forest roads and tracks, and I believe this activity is closely linked to levels of hunger and, in the male, to establishing and patrolling territories.

The remaining ten per cent covers the active periods in the tiger's life, and it is these that I will now describe in some detail. The observations recorded here have been gathered over a period of nine years, and none have been easily come by. For centuries sportsmen and naturalists have sought to get close to the tiger, but very rarely does this elusive predator oblige. It seems appropriate, therefore, to begin with a part of the tiger's life that has very rarely been seen, let alone documented; an intimate part of the tiger's life, which Fateh saw in its entirety for the first time in 1985 – after 17 years of tiger watching experience.

COURTSHIP AND MATING

The process of courtship and mating starts with the tigress coming into oestrus, and on the three occasions on which I have witnessed this stage the behaviour pattern has been identical. The female becomes restless, very vocal, and very mobile.

My first encounter happened early one morning. I was listening intently for sounds of alarm in the forest when I heard a long moan, repeated at regular intervals. I followed the sound and found a tigress walking down the road. In the 45 minutes that I kept pace behind her she vocalized some 30 times, and spray-marked trees or rubbed herself on the bushes some 25 times. The forest echoed with her long wails, peacocks flew off in alarm, and at one time a group of sambar bellowed at her in panic before fleeing away. She was completely unconcerned and walked along briskly, stopping to spray a tree or rub her haunches on patches of grass or bush. Sometimes she would rub her neck high against the trunk of a tree. I was mesmerized by her total obsession with her physical condition. She was using all her energies in this regular vocalization and incessant marking so as to attract any male tiger in the vicinity. Even if a male passed the area later he would be able to smell her scent and follow her. Eventually I lost sight of her as she disappeared into a thick ravine.

Like all predators, tigers spend much of their time at rest, conserving their energy. In the forests of Ranthambhore they favour the numerous areas of tall grass. Each tiger has a number of regular resting places, strategically placed near water-holes and on routes used by deer and other prey species. Here the tiger sits or sleeps, ever alert to the slightest sound or movement and ready to attack at a moment's notice.

LEFT Even when fast asleep, the tiger's senses are monitoring every sound and movement in the forest around it. The soft whirring of a tiny blue kingfisher's wings is enough to make Noon blink her eyes open. She watches lazily for a moment – then sleeps again, waiting for the evening when the deer will come down to the pool to drink.

LEFT Tigers vary a great deal in their choice of resting place. Some choose deep cover while others lie out in the minimal cover of a rock or bush, or even out in the open. Here the Bakaula male rests in the cool shade of a dense jamun grove.

BELOW LEFT In the 47°C heat of Ranthambhore's summer, Kublai seeks relief by spending a large part of the day half-immersed in a water-hole. Though powerful swimmers and quite at home in the water, tigers appear to dislike getting their faces wet.

TOP RIGHT The day's sleeping and resting is over. As the sun sinks, Laxmi stirs and begins her evening grooming. She may spend 30 minutes or more working her rough tongue over paws, chest and other parts of her body in a ritual that nearly always indicates that the tiger is about to move off.

RIGHT Grooming is usually followed by a spell of yawning, and in this photograph of Noon a huge yawn reveals that the tigress has broken her right upper canine – probably in the course of making a kill.

Sometimes the intense marking and vocalization of a tigress will attract a single male. On other occasions more than one tiger might appear, especially if their movement patterns have overlapped, and in this situation a vicious fight can break out over the female. One of the most exciting accounts of such an encounter was recorded by P. Hanley in his book *Tiger Trails in Assam* (1961). Hanley found a tigress vocalizing with great regularity. This soon attracted a male tiger who cautiously started his approach, but before he could get close enough another male arrived and promptly attacked the first. It was a bloody fight and the two tigers seem to have wrestled standing on their hindlegs, clawing and attempting to bite each other, and roaring viciously. One of them succeeded in tearing the other's neck open with a slash of its claws. The battle was savage and one of the tigers soon departed from the fray, bleeding and limping badly.

Hanley now observed a third male tiger watching the fight from behind a bush. The victor also had great weals across his ribs where he had been torn by the claws of his opponent. He rolled around in a patch of grass, wiping the blood away, and then approached the tigress. As he came to within a few

ABOVE After yawning, a tiger will nearly always rise and start to move. Here, the large male Genghis allows himself one last yawn before moving off to walk his territory. Males tend to have larger ranges than females and consequently spend much more of their time walking.

paces of her the third male sprang towards him. The exhausted victor was no match for the third tiger and was easily chased away. Soon the tigress and the third male bounded away into the forest. The tigress had sat quietly throughout observing the aggressive conflict over her.

Be it through such a struggle or where a single male finds a tigress in oestrus, the normal period that a male will spend with the female is between three and seven days, when the tigress is at her most receptive. Sometimes that can be stretched to a couple of weeks. I have seen much courting during my nine years observing tigers but unfortunately no mating. In the first instance, in March 1981, I saw a male and female sitting over a sambar kill at 7.00 a.m. The female was keeping close to the remains of the kill in an effort to protect it from crows and vultures. The male was 30 metres beyond, sitting near a bush. After some 20 minutes he rose, sniffed the trunk of a tree, rubbed his neck on a spot on the tree, and followed this by lifting his forepaw and clawing that spot repeatedly. He then sniffed it again and hung out his tongue, which is the way tigers react on sniffing their own or another tiger's scent. He then made his way towards the female and sat about seven

TOP Having groomed herself, yawned, and had a good look around, Nick Ear stretches her powerful body before setting off to check her beat.

ABOVE A tigress in oestrus will cover great distances, constantly vocalizing and spray-marking in an effort to attract a mate. Here, Noon pauses in one of the hundreds of *nallahs* or dry stream beds that criss-cross the forest.

PREVIOUS PAGES Noon paces along a forest road during oestrus. In Ranthambhore she will be almost certain to mate, but where tiger populations are low and widely dispersed, a tigress is sometimes unable to find a mate despite her frenzied activities.

RIGHT Late one afternoon we came across Genghis, a magnificent male tiger, resting close to the road. He roused, yawned, and then leisurely followed the jeep down the road, spray-marking as he went. He had just moved into the area and was asserting his territorial claim.

Noon pauses for a brief rest close to Jogi Mahal. But there is little peace for her in the oestrus period and soon she will be on the move again — constantly vocalizing, spray-marking and rubbing her body against trees and bushes.

metres away from her. After another 15 minutes he came closer still, sniffed her rear and then proceeded to lick her back and side until he reached her face, which he licked all over. The tigress in the meantime had her eyes closed as if in some kind of ecstasy. There was no vocalization. The male then sat just behind her but much to my frustration they both rose a few minutes later and strolled away into the forest and out of sight.

In February 1984, again at 7.00 a.m., a male tiger was found close to Jogi Mahal in the company of two females. The male was sitting near the first female and about 30 metres away sat a second female. The male soon rose, nuzzled the first female who was smaller in size, and licked her face. This courtship activity was rudely interrupted by the second female who ran in closer in an attempt to push the courting female away. But the male, coughing sharply, mock-charged her and she moved back a little. The male then rose with the first female and walked around a part of Padam Talao, followed at a distance by the other female. They entered a dry stream bed and, behind a bush, amidst much vocalization, they mated, observed at a distance by the second female.

The next morning all three were encounterd at the other side of the lake at about 7.30 a.m. The male was sitting in a clearing away from his chosen female. The second tigress sat 60 metres away, watching. She made two advances towards the courting couple, only to be rebuffed by the male. Shortly afterwards the first female attempted to secure the male's undivided attention through a range of acrobatics. Twice she got up and walked up a slight incline, after which she rolled back down, reaching the male who bared his canines viciously at her. She moaned loudly and in a submissive posture rolled on her back, her feet towards the sky.

All of this was recorded by a tracker in the forest; I have never seen tigers mating. Fateh, who has now spent 17 years in the forest of Ranthambhore, saw tigers mating for the first time on 9 April 1985. I had unfortunately left by then. But before describing this remarkable episode, it is worthwhile going back to March when the two tigers seem to have met.

My diary notes for 6/7 March record that the large male tiger Kublai spent most of that 48-hour period in the vicinity of the lakes, and that pug mark evidence indicated the presence, with him, of the resident female Noon. It was the beginning of a long courtship, which we were to observe with mounting excitement and tension over a period of more than a month.

Every day we set out eagerly to search for evidence of the pair. Often we would find them together, sometimes lying contentedly a few metres apart, at other times nuzzling each other about the face. Sometimes we watched them interacting over sambar kills near the shores of the lake. And on one memorable occasion they indulged in a mock fight — an incredible sight as these two magnificent animals reared up on their hindlegs, Kublai growling as he gently boxed Noon about the neck and head.

As the days passed the pair became very vocal, often filling the night air with the widest range of growls, cries and moans I have ever heard. Kublai's interest seemed to be growing day by day. More and more frequently we would observe him nuzzling Noon or, when the two were apart, sniffing the ground where she had walked or rested. Their interactions seemed to be increasing in intensity all the time.

We could scarcely believe our good fortune. The pair remained in the area of the lakes throughout the rest of March and into April, providing us with a unique opportunity to observe the entire courtship without interruption. But the suspense was almost unbearable. None of us had ever seen the final act in this drama. Our one thought as we set off each morning was, 'Will this be the day?' But the days passed, and on 6 April, after 30 days of continuous observation, my time ran out and I was forced to leave Ranthambhore. Fateh's detailed notes provide us with a graphic account of the final chapter in this story.

The morning of 9 April is dark and stormy. Thick black clouds billow across the sky and a blustery wind kicks up swirls of dust along the shore of Rajbagh. A sambar carcass is floating in one of the pools, but there are no signs of tigers. Satisfied that Kublai and Noon are not in the immediate area,

From 6 March to 9 April 1985 Kublai and Noon spent much of their time together. It was the preliminary phase of their courtship, and much of their interaction was over food.

LEFT 1.20 p.m., 10 March, and Noon drags ashore the carcass of a sambar hind she has killed in the shallows of Padam Talao. She has retained her vice-like grip on the throat, and the sambar's body trails between her forelegs and beneath her body. Once ashore she pulled the carcass into long grass 100m back from the lake in order to feed.

BELOW LEFT 4.00 p.m Noon returns to the lake to quench her thirst and to soak in the cool water. Tigers will often do this soon after making a kill, and also during feeding, particularly in hot weather. Noon is even more fond of the water than most and is often seen partly immersed.

BELOW 4.20 p.m Noon suddenly rushes from the water and charges back to her kill, clearing a deep muddy wallow with one five-metre leap. She had probably seen a greedy tree-pie heading for the meat!

7.30 p.m. A deep resonant 'aaoon' reverberates across the lake, soon followed by another. Kublai is moving towards Noon. Tiger sounds echo off the walls of the fort for another 20 minutes. Has Noon invited Kublai to the feast? Or has the male's appearance some days ago stimulated the tigress's oestrus cycle?

6.45 a.m., 11 March. Noon is sitting some ten metres outside the grass and we suspect that Kublai has taken over her kill. She rises and moves tentatively towards the grass, but retreats again submissively in the face of a series of low rumbling growls. Later in the day she tries to stalk another sambar but is unsuccessful, and for the rest of the day is kept away from the kill by Kublai who remains in the grass, not even coming down to the lake to drink.

During this preliminary courtship, Kublai annexed at least four of Noon's kills, and only once was she able to snatch part of one back – while Kublai was taking a drink at the lake. He was firmly established as the dominant male and Noon's food intake suffered considerably.

Fateh drives back to the resthouse, content to try again later. At four in the afternoon a radio message comes through, telling of alarm calls in the area of Rajbagh. Fateh rushes back to the lake, and to the small pool where the carcass is lying. By now a gale is blowing. Covered with a film of dust he seeks the shelter of some trees.

At 5.20 p.m. Noon emerges from a thicket of grass and sits at the edge. She is soon followed by Kublai who reclines some metres away. Both tigers appear relaxed. Quite suddenly Noon rises and strides rapidly to Kublai, who raises his head. Noon rubs her flank against him in an effort to get him to rise. He does, and she quickly settles in front of him, offering him her rear quarters. Immediately, Kublai mounts her and some 15 seconds later Noon growls sharply, followed by a few lower-pitched growls for another 10 seconds. Then Kublai jumps off and Noon, after a sharp grunt, stands up and moves away. They both go and rest some metres away. Eleven minutes later Noon rises again and moves quickly towards Kublai, seductively rubbing her head, and then her right flank, against his mouth. She then sits in front of him. Kublai stands again and mounts her. This time they are partially hidden by the grass thicket. Noon emits a sharp grunt and in 30

9 April 1985 saw Fateh's 17 years of painstaking observation rewarded when he was able to watch, and record on film, the culmination of Kublai's month-long courtship of Noon.

LEFT 5.30 p.m. Kublai and Noon have already mated twice, but partly hidden in the dense grass. They now laze at the edge of the thicket indulging in protracted love-play. Noon nuzzles Kublai, they rub heads, and Kublai's paws touch the tigress's chest. She is standing while he remains sprawled on his side as she tries persistently to rouse him.

BELOW LEFT 5.37 p.m. Kublai leaves the grass and strolls off round the lake followed by Noon who at one point overtakes him and leads the way. But their attention is caught by a sambar carcass floating in the water. They make no attempt to rush in and drag it out, but the presence of food so near brings their walk to an end and they remain on the shore nearby.

RIGHT 5.45 p.m. Noon moves quickly to Kublai's side and with a brief nuzzling movement along his head and neck she brushes her flank against him seductively. By this time Noon was forcing a response from the male every 15 minutes or so in her eagerness to mate.

seconds Kublai jumps off the snarling tigress.

Now Kublai moves right out of the grass and slowly walks around the edge of the lake. He pauses to stretch himself on the fallen trunk of a palm tree, and then walks on the trunk before moving to the edge of the water, close to the sambar carcass. He snarls viciously at a couple of crocodiles attempting to nibble at the carcass, and then settles down to watch against a backdrop of the red flowering tree, the 'flame of the forest', with the flowers scattered around him on the grass. Fateh is astonished at the raw beauty of the scene from across the pool. Tiger, red flowers and sambar carcass are all reflected in the water, creating images of poetic intensity.

Noon quickly follows Kublai's path to the edge of the water. With a sharp snarl at a gliding crocodile she encourages a response from Kublai by nuzzling him, sliding her flank against his and then sitting receptively at the edge of the water less than a metre in front of him. Kublai rises, seemingly aroused again by Noon's provocative position. He mounts her, sliding his forepaws down her back until they make contact with the ground near her forelegs. His head leans against the right side of her neck as if they were entwined. His hindlegs remain half bent as his forelegs straddle Noon's neck. Her forelegs are fully stretched and the hindlegs slightly bent. After 15 seconds Noon emits a sharp growl and Kublai grips the folds of skin around

RIGHT 5.48 p.m. Noon has moved in front of Kublai and dropped into a receptive crouch. Immediately he moves into position over her.

RIGHT 5.49 p.m. The pair mate; Kublai gripping the loose folds of skin on the side of Noon's neck with his canines. Coitus lasts some 15 seconds.

ABOVE The act is interrupted violently by Noon as she twists and snarls aggressively at the male, throwing him off before mating is completed.

LEFT 6.12 p.m Yet another period of copulation takes place, despite the fact that Kublai has seen us and is watching us carefully. This time he does not grip her neck, and Noon is not aggressive; she lies at full stretch, her chin almost on the ground. Tigers copulate with some frequency and in this case the pair mated eight times between 5.20 and 6.48 p.m.

A rarely seen example of the violent aggression that often accompanies the end of the sexual act. With a vicious snarl Noon twists her body right round and lashes upwards at Kublai with her right forepaw. Just in time he jerks his head clear of the tigress's claws.

the nape of her neck. Some seconds later she throws him off, snarling upwards aggressively. Carefully they lick every inch of their rears, especially their genitals. Fifteen minutes later Noon initiates another session of copulation in much the same way. The sun has set and the forest sounds change as the crickets take over. Way out in the distance a brown fishing owl flies off in search of prey, and a pair of golden orioles flits across the sky, the bright yellow of their chests providing relief against a dull forest green.

Now Noon walks off around the edge of the lake. Kublai decides to follow, but he has gone only a few metres when the crocodiles return to the carcass and he decides to retrace his steps. Amidst much snarling he settles down at the edge of the water looking carefully at the carcass some three or four metres away. Noon is out of sight. After five minutes Kublai rises again as if to follow her, but the crocodile activity again forces him to retrace his steps. He seems caught between staying around the carcass and being with Noon. The light is slowly fading but minutes later Noon returns; again she rubs bodies with Kublai and they mate.

Kublai's interest in the sambar carcass is much greater than Noon's. She seems not in the least bothered about food. In the next half hour they mate

ABOVE In the last few weeks before her cubs are born, the tigress retreats into remote parts of the forest and into deep cover where she will select a cave or other natural enclosure in which to give birth. At this stage she is ruthless and aggressive, and this, combined with her secrecy, is why we have never yet seen cubs younger than four months old.

three more times. It looks unreal as their perfect reflections glint off the water. Night is slowly taking over. The time is 6.48 p.m. Fateh has watched eight copulations in 88 minutes. It has been his most exciting observation ever of tiger behaviour. Awed by the power and beauty of the scene he slowly drives back to Jogi Mahal. The next day there is no trace of the tigers. The saga is over. Thirty-five days of regular interaction culminated finally in the mating of Kublai and Noon.

Observations of matings are rare, and very seldom recorded. Tigers obviously prefer a quiet privacy, free from the disturbance of human observers. In Ranthambhore, records show that mating occurs at all times of the year, with no definite or intense mating season. The tigress who conceives may not come into oestrus again for 18-22 months, though there are exceptions to this. She spends a long period of time teaching and training her cubs. Those who do not conceive, or who lose their litters for some reason, will come into oestrus again anywhere between one month and three months later. However, these records are from zoos, and very little information is available on the tiger oestrus cycle in the wild.

MOTHER AND YOUNG

The gestation period is not known exactly, but captive records indicate a period of 93-110 days. It is difficult to spot a pregnant tigress in the wild as the bulge of her belly is visible only during the last ten to twelve days of pregnancy. However, she is heavy and must find a sufficient intake of food. Hanley recorded an exceptional observation in Assam. He found a tigress, heavily pregnant and lying in tall elephant grass at the edge of a tea estate. For two weeks a male tiger would bring her portions of kills, and when he arrived he would call out to her with a strange cry as if asking her to come out and start eating. The tigress had quadruplets.

In the last few days of her pregnancy a tigress which you may have been observing quite regularly, suddenly disappears from sight. I have tried desperately to record this mystery period, which starts ten to fifteen days before delivery and continues until the cubs are four to six months old. I have tried to put together a possible description of this period from evidence of pug marks, actual sightings by trackers and patrolling parties, and from indications of kills occurring regularly in specific areas. But despite all our

RIGHT A brown fishing owl peers down from his roost in the forest — one of the very few silent observers likely to catch a glimpse of tiger cubs in their first few weeks of life. But even here lies a threat. The tigress must be ever-alert to the danger from above as several birds of prey are capable of carrying away a helpless cub.

efforts in Ranthambhore we have never yet seen a tigress with cubs under the age of four to five months.

As the time of the delivery approaches, the tigress begins to look, and no doubt feel, increasingly vulnerable. Her swollen belly must make hunting difficult, and at the same time she is becoming more and more preoccupied with finding a safe place in which to give birth. It may be a cave, a natural rock overhang, or thick bush with dense cover all around. She will spend most of her time in the vicinity of the den, familiarizing herself with every nook and corner of the terrain, including details of animal movement and water supply. The spot chosen by her must not only have sufficient prey around, or within easy striking range, but also be well protected so as to conceal her cubs from predators, be they on the ground or in the sky.

Zoo records indicate that a litter of cubs can be born within an hour, but sometimes the birth takes as long as 24 hours. The process no doubt is painful and exhausting and at this time the tigress gets some nourishment from the placenta and embryonic sac, which she invariably eats. The cubs are born blind and in a rather helpless state. It takes anything from three to fourteen days for the eyes to open, though full vision is not acquired until some weeks later. Both zoo records and observations in the wild indicate that a tigress may deliver up to six or seven cubs in a litter, and that the ratio of the sexes at birth is one to one.

Unable to see, the young cubs tend to stay in the security of the den with the tigress, who now becomes a committed, caring, and ruthlessly protective mother. This close association continues for some two years, but the early days are devoted entirely to the helpless cubs as she spends most of her time suckling them. There are no records of how long the suckling continues in the wild, or at what point it is supplemented by meat, but I think it must continue for over three months. I think that after the first few days following the delivery the tigress will move out to hunt so as to eat and give herself some nourishment after the difficult days she has been through. I also think she must attempt to kill as near to her den as possible, so as never to be drawn too far away from the young.

These hunting forays must be nerve-racking times for the tigress, with half her mind always on the safety of her cubs. Their mortality rate is highest at this time, and if ever a tigress is encountered in this state she will be aggressive and may even charge to kill. And this is not only in the face of other predators or scavengers, but also with human intruders. K. Anderson, while hunting in Madras, wrote in *Man-eaters and Jungle Killers* (1957) of, 'A shelving rock which met the rising ground at an angle of perhaps thirty degrees, forming a shallow recess rather than a real cave. Two large balls of russet brown, striped with black, white underneath, were tumbling over one another in a vigorous game of 'catch-as-catch can'. They were two tiger cubs, and they were playing. I stopped in my tracks, the only movement being an imperceptible cocking of the rifle, with the faintest of clicks. But it was enough. They stopped playing, disentangled themselves, and looked at me in alarm. One with a look of innocent surprise and the other with its features wrinkled to emit a hiss of consternation.

'That hiss was the signal for all hell to break loose, for it awoke the tigress, who was sleeping. With a series of shattering roars she dashed out of the cavern, vaulted over the cubs and came straight at me. The distance may have been twenty yards. I covered her between the eyes as she advanced. Then, five yards away, she stopped. She crouched with her belly to the ground, eyes blazing and mouth wide, while her roars and snarls shook the very ground on which I stood.

'Wonder of wonders, she had not charged home. Her courage had failed her at the last moment. She was telling me, in the simplest of languages, "Get out quickly, and don't harm my cubs or I will kill you." Step by step I retreated backwards, while never removing my eyes from her, never allowing the rifle sights to waver in the slightest, my forefinger still on the trigger. And she remained where she was. It was as if she understood that I was going.'

I know of three occasions in the last five years where patrolling parties in Ranthambhore have had a fleeting glimpse of a tigress with tiny cubs tucked away in thick bush with high grass around. In each case they have been aggressively charged by the furious mother and have only escaped by the skin of their teeth.

Any intrusion into the area around her cubs is treated by the tigress with great suspicion, and if disturbed she is likely to change her den by carrying her helpless cubs in her mouth, holding them by the head with her canines and molars and shifting them one by one. She is alone in providing this protection and security, doing the job efficiently and with great care.

Tiger cubs in their first few months are vulnerable and their mortality rate is high, sometimes over 50 per cent, so all the attention of the mother goes into keeping them alive and fit. Endless time must be spent by her in licking and cleaning the cubs to promote better circulation or bowel movement. As the days roll by and the cubs grow, they become frisky, starting limited exploratory drives around their den and playing with leaves, branches and anything else around. The mother must now instill some order and discipline in them. She also starts to carry meat back to the den for them and I have followed drag marks of a chital nearly one-and-a-half kilometres from where it was killed before losing it in a thick gorge. Unlike the lion, a tigress will open up a kill for her cubs, but rarely eats first.

All this activity continues without the presence of a father, as the male who fathered the litter leaves immediately after mating. Most of the time, while her cubs are young, the tigress must protect them from other male tigers as there have been several occasions when males have killed young male cubs and this probably occurs as the male senses future competition for space and territory. Inglis (1892) heard of an instance where a mauled cub was found at the site of a fight between a male and female, and Smeeton (1961) reported a similar fight where two cubs were killed. He states, 'As far as we could read the tracks, a tiger and the tigress with her two cubs had come into the jungle and had met the big tiger, but who had actually killed the cubs, and why, we couldn't tell.' However, not all authors agree on this point. Sainthill Eardley Wilmot in his book *Forest Life and Sport in India* (1910), takes another view. 'The male tiger does not seem to be addicted to infanticide, though when they are in confinement this crime is reported as not uncommon: in fact I have seen him in company with cubs of all ages and it is probably the difficulty of finding food for many voracious mouths that ultimately enforces a separation.'

In Ranthambhore, very rarely does one come across records or evidence of fatal interaction between tigers. Maybe these do occur, but very seldom can one prove it as the natural cycle of a forest destroys all evidence, burying it in the earth. Ranthambhore in all these years provided just one example of mortal combat and we attempt to relate this from evidence we discovered the morning after it happened.

There was a full moon on the night of 10 November 1981 when a tigress with two cubs appears to have been walking down the Lahpur valley nearly 20 kilometres from Jogi Mahal. Suddenly she must have spotted an adult male tiger walking in the opposite direction. Indications exist of the cubs scampering away. The tigress seems to have continued towards the tiger and there were marks where both sat down in the middle of the road. They must have then risen and gone to sit in the sandy part of a nearby stream bed. Obviously at this moment the tigress was trying her level best to be affectionate with the male and bid him a rapid farewell before any interaction was possible between him and the cubs. But it did not work. Apparently the cubs attempted to scamper back to their mother, probably finding the insecurity of separation too much to take.

At this moment there must have been havoc, and some incredible vocalization was even heard in a guard post some two kilometres away. It appears that the male must have moved, in a flash, towards the cubs, and the mother was forced to take lightning action. With a leap and a bound she attacked the male from the rear, clawing his right foreleg before sinking her canines in and killing him. It was an amazing example of instinctive reaction: a tigress killing a prime male tiger to save her cubs from possible death. The male must have been caught completely by surprise by the attack, and just succumbed. Later, the tigress proceeded to open his rump, and eat off his left hindleg. Tiger eating tiger: this was a rare example of a fatal interaction between tigers.

Such is the skill of the tigress that the first few months of her cubs' lives are shrouded in mystery. In nine years of watching tigers I have hardly ever seen the pug marks of a tigress with cubs younger than about four or five months. Before that age they are kept hidden away in deep cover, and never venture into clearings or on to the forest roads. Between the ages of two and three months the cubs make their first limited explorations around the immediate vicinity of the den – closely supervised by the mother. From three months onwards they probably venture a little farther each day, but still these movements will be carefully supervised, and almost certainly take place entirely under the cloak of darkness. It is a time when the tigress is sharply alert to any danger, and she walks keeping her cubs closely bunched together around her. She is now at her most dangerous, because in addition to protecting her cubs she is also teaching them the ways of the forest. It is a time when she must use different shelters each night depending on the degree of movement. It is the cubs' first experience of the forest which is to be their future home.

RIGHT Rarely is it possible to photograph a tiger family together. Here, a tigress rests in a dry stream bed accompanied by her four cubs. One has dashed out of the frame, seeking cover in the grass. Another hesitates. A third moves toward the safety of the mother and the dominant cub lying beside her. Even though nearly 12 months old the cubs are very wary, and in 10 minutes the family had disappeared into cover.

RIGHT Padmini's litter of 1976. Akbar, the dominant cub, lies asleep in the foreground. Babar and Hamir watch warily from higher up. Laxmi's flank is just visible on the left. All these tigers survived to maturity and then split up to establish their own ranges. This photograph of the cubs took many months of patient tracking and searching by Fateh.

ABOVE Two cubs from Padmini's second litter begin the transition to independence. They are 18 months old and Padmini has left them to fend for themselves for a few days. She will return briefly to ensure a minimum amount of food is available – but this is the critical period in which the cubs must put into practice their mother's months of teaching.

GLIMPSES OF FAMILY LIFE

At about six months old the cubs start to roam around more freely. They are now the size of Alsatian dogs and the tigress moves them greater distances, her hunting range expanding considerably as the young ones familiarize themselves with various landmarks, watch and observe prey and the way their mother stalks, kills and eats, explore water-holes and learn about the forest. The tigress is now obsessed not only with the training of her cubs but also with the procurement of food. The cubs are growing fast, their increased appetites need a constant source of food and, depending on the size of the litter, the mother needs to kill every day or every other day. The cubs are not mature enough to help her in this activity and only tend to get in the way of her hunting, not giving her a moment's peace. It is during this period that she instills discipline through the occasional slap and a sharp growl, and it is through a complex series of sounds that the cubs are trained to avoid danger and to remain quiet when she hunts.

In December 1976 Fateh discovered a tigress whom he called Padmini, and much to his delight found that she was accompanied by five cubs. This discovery caused great excitement because very rarely in the past had a tigress been seen with such a large brood. Such was the rarity of this event that Fateh made a determined effort to observe Padmini and her young. Her movements were concentrated in the Lakarda valley from where, only recently, a village had been shifted with all its cattle. In years past this was a most unlikely place to find tigers as the disturbance of the inhabitants kept the animals away. But Lakarda was now deserted, and with nature regenerating itself as the animals returned it seemed quite fitting that Padmini and her cubs were frequenting the area.

Now, patiently following her pug marks, Fateh played a game of hide-and-seek with Padmini for nearly a month until the tension broke. Sitting late one evening near the deserted village, Fateh was waiting for sounds of tiger activity. An icy wind blew and the crickets chattered in abandon when suddenly the chilling death cry of a buffalo shattered the night. Fateh rushed towards the sound to find a large tigress caught in his jeep lights, snarling furiously and backing off her kill. In the glare of the lights he caught a fleeting glimpse of five cubs behind her. Fateh left, not wishing to disturb the situation, and returned at dawn. Some distance away Padmini lay by her kill, so he quickly climbed up a tree to observe the day's proceedings. The buffalo was a lame animal that the villagers had left behind, and now a part of the rump was eaten. There was no sign of the cubs. Meat is precious, and Padmini sat protecting the carcass from scavengers, herself eating briefly at noon. She was alert and aggressive to the initial clicks of the camera, charging the tree on which Fateh sat. But slowly she relaxed.

Late in the afternoon the distinct alarm calls of jackals warned Fateh that the cubs were on the move, and he glimpsed them briefly before a sharp cough from the tigress scattered them into the forest. For the next four days Fateh watched the tigress on her lonely vigil as the carcass gradually diminished. The cubs only came in to eat at night after he left. But Padmini sat on guard, chasing the occasional crow or tree-pie that ventured too close. Not a scrap of meat would be wasted.

As the month went by, our sightings of the cubs became more frequent and we found that there were three males and two females. One of the females was in poor condition and lagging behind. She was obviously getting the smallest share of the meat – but what a task for Padmini, to hunt and kill for such a large brood, now needing at least 20-30 kilogrammes of meat a day. By the following month there was no sign of the small female and I felt sure that nature must have taken its course. Survival is only of the fittest, and feeding five cubs is no easy task. One had obviously passed into the arms of nature. This age of six to eight months is very tough.

Our sightings of this family continued to become more regular but Padmini spent much time trying to prevent us from seeing her cubs. In fact twice she led us off in pursuit of her, so providing an opportunity for her cubs to evade us. But now we had a marvellous opportunity to observe the growing-up process. We called the three males Akbar, Babar and Hamir and the female Laxmi. Akbar was the most confident of the cubs and always came the closest to us, followed by Babar and Hamir and then Laxmi.

Late one evening we spotted the family sitting by the side of a road some seven kilometres from Lakarda. Akbar was sitting boldly in front, with Padmini sleeping near Laxmi behind him. Our presence heralded some interaction, with Laxmi getting up and nuzzling her mother, and Padmini returning this gesture with a few licks. Babar and Hamir played in the distance, circling each other and mock pawing. Akbar rose suddenly and, in a few bounds, leapt towards his brothers. Hamir rose in anticipation and they greeted each other – both rising on their hind feet and boxing each other gently with their forepaws.

Fateh decided it was time to observe the behaviour of the family around a kill and a buffalo was brought and turned loose close by the tigers. Padmini moved in a flash, but instead of killing it she chose to disable it with a blow on its hind quarters. She then withdrew and sat a little distance away. The buffalo, now slightly injured, limped around in front of the tigers. Very cautiously Akbar and Hamir approached it, but the buffalo charged them and they rushed away into high grass. Again they emerged, with Babar and Laxmi following, taking four positions to encircle the buffalo. But whenever the cubs tried to go in close they were charged, and this little scene lasted for 30 minutes while Padmini looked on. Suddenly Akbar leapt towards the buffalo, landing on its hind quarters and bringing it down. After several clumsy movements he sank his canines into the animal's neck. Hamir now entered the fray and sat on the rump. Soon they started eating, but after some 20 minutes Padmini rose and moved them off, walking towards Babar and Laxmi and nudging them as if to say, 'Come on, it's your turn.' But shyer than their brothers, they did not get up and Padmini started feeding. Padmini was not only allowing the cubs to learn how to kill but also ensuring the equal sharing of food.

The next morning very little remained of the carcass and soon Padmini rose and with much nuzzling moved her cubs away. As they walked the cubs tried to rub their bodies against each other. For us it had been a most rewarding incident.

This method of training the young has been recorded by many observers, among them F.C. Hicks who states in his book *Forty Years Among the Wild Animals of India* (1910), 'If cubs are present, the hind leg of the kill will frequently be found to be broken, the idea being to disable the animal and then to play with it alive for the edification of the cubs, while the nose, ears and eyes will invariably be found much gnawed and torn by the cubs.'

As the months rolled by we found the cubs accepting our presence with greater confidence, particularly Akbar who would always approach the jeep and sit some six or seven metres away. By the age of about 17 months we saw the four cubs on their own more and more frequently. Padmini's presence became very irregular; she would absent herself for a few days and then return. The critical lesson had begun. Even though not proficient in killing, the time had come for the cubs to fend for themselves. With Padmini absent, Akbar took over the leadership of the group. He was the dominant male and was now in charge of his siblings. Padmini would appear every few days so as to ensure the availability of food, but then she would disappear. Her absences became longer.

Akbar would now command the movement of the others through sound, but he was seldom in close proximity to them. Even when sitting they would be much more spread out, and aggressive snarls were frequently heard between the brothers. But all three males would nuzzle and lick Laxmi. The breaking-up process between them had begun, and one day while watching them in a patch of grass we realized there was no sign of Akbar. He had gone off to find a life for himself. He was around 21 months old when he left, and we saw him several times on his own. Hamir followed a month and a half later, but Babar and Laxmi remained together for yet another two months. In a way they seemed to have a closer bond, a more dependent relationship.

All four tigers were now launched on the critical process of independent living, learning to move through separate ranges and putting their mother's training to the test. It was now difficult to locate them easily; all pug marks and indications were those of single tigers. It was like looking for a needle in a haystack. Later we found Padmini with two more litters; once in the middle of 1979 and again in the middle of 1982. In the years between 1976 and 1982 she raised ten young.

In 1981 we came upon Laxmi with a litter, the cubs again somewhere between five and seven months. She had three young ones and they were resting in the grass around the third lake. It was a heart-warming sight on that March evening. Playfully, two of the cubs reared their bodies, attempting to swat each other. Then followed a chase through the tall grass. The third cub approached his mother, licked her on the nose and stroked her head. Close behind came the two leaping cubs, who banged into the third one. They all entwined themselves with Laxmi, nuzzling and rubbing bodies. One of the cubs suddenly moved off and leapt into the air, falling on his forepaws as if making an effort to jump on a mouse or bird. Quite suddenly another cub pounced into a bush from which four partridges flew out. They soon joined Laxmi again and one of the cubs licked her on the mouth. Laxmi coughed and affectionately swatted one of the more frisky ones. All three then played around amidst soft grunts. Soon, a little tired, they rested near the mother, two of them trying to sleep.

All in all it was a spectacular year, and though our observations were mostly late in the evening or early in the morning, and very seldom with enough light to document them on film, we had, for the first time, encountered what must have been the father figure enjoying the company of his mate and young. It happened one evening when we found Laxmi's family in the company of a male. Whenever the male walked towards the cubs they would jump up and nuzzle him and he would lick them; an incredible display of affection from a male tiger. On another occasion the male was found in the grass eating the rump of a sambar, in which activity he was joined by one of

OVERLEAF Kublai strides purposefully along a forest road, spray-marking and scratching trees in the never-ending business of asserting his territorial claims and warning off any would-be usurpers.

the cubs. To our surprise they ate together quite peacefully.

Males associating with a tigress and her cubs have been observed before, but always as a rarity. George Schaller in 1965 saw a large male tiger with a female and four cubs, first when the cubs were four months old and then again when they were about eleven months old. Billy Arjun Singh, in his book *Tiger Tiger*, observed a male tiger amicably sharing a kill with a female and three cubs.

The question of whether or not tigers climb trees is an interesting one. In *Wild Animals in Central India* (1923), A.A. Dunbar Brander states, 'Tigers seldom attempt to climb trees but they can do this to a much greater extent than is generally supposed. I firmly believe they can certainly get up a branched tree at which they can rush. The number of fatal accidents are evidence of this. I do not think a large heavy tiger could climb a smooth limbless tree, but tigresses and smaller tigers can get up a tree with only a small amount of assistance from side branches.'

Once, while we were watching Laxmi and her three cubs, one of the youngsters suddenly walked up to a tree, climbed a metre or two up the trunk, and went and sat on the first overhanging branch. Above him sat a peacock, which he watched curiously as the peacock called in alarm.

On another occasion Laxmi's family was well hidden in the grass of the meadow around Malik Talao. A group of chital including a young fawn were grazing with some nilgai, oblivious of the tigers. Laxmi started stalking with considerable skill and came quite close to the chital mother. But suddenly she was spotted and within seconds the chital dashed off in great leaps, followed unsuccessfully by Laxmi. The nilgai escaped, but the fawn in all this confusion ran straight towards the hidden cubs and the dominant cub leapt out and gave a kind of circular chase, covering some 300 metres before he leapt successfully on to the fawn and killed it.

His chase was followed hesitantly by his two siblings, but much to their dismay he quickly picked up the fawn and rushed some 300 metres away to eat in the cover of a thick bush. Soon the other two cubs approached him, but again he fled into thicker forest as if asserting his right to consume the whole animal as he had so expertly killed it. Eventually they were all lost to view. Laxmi remained throughout, sitting quietly in the meadow waiting for the next herd of deer to arrive. The cubs at this point must have been twelve to fourteen months old.

My last moments with this family were in the presence of a mature male and on one occasion we saw him carrying a large chital doe into a stream bed, followed by Laxmi and her three cubs. I had a feeling then that he must have contributed significantly in providing food for the family. By 1982 the family group had broken up to go their separate ways.

From these descriptions of family life it seems that tigers have an exceedingly close-knit bond with each other while they grow up, and that the mother plays a role of total devotion in this process — sacrificing all so that her cubs may survive. Sometimes the bond between tiger and tigress can be strong enough for them both to be involved in raising the family, but this is the exception and not the rule.

THE TIGER'S RANGE AND MOBILITY

The focal point of Laxmi's movement pattern is this water-hole in Lakarda valley. Like most females she has a relatively small range.

What happens to the young ones when they reach the stage of independence and break away? To answer this we must go back to Padmini's first litter. Padmini herself had a large range in which she moved during 1977/8. It stretched over approximately 45 square kilometres. Her female cub Laxmi has spent the last five years in an area of 15 square kilometres, which includes part of Padmini's original range. It stretched from the third lake to Lakarda and Kachida, although Laxmi focused her activity regularly around Lakarda. Akbar seems to have had an area of 20-30 square kilometres, again stretching from the third lake to Lakarda and up to the edge of Bakaula, and in this area he was the dominant male. Babar was sighted irregularly and Hamir had shifted to the area behind the fort, called Nalghati, but again sightings were irregular and I do not have any idea of his movement patterns.

ABOVE Noon makes good use of
a narrow animal path as she
heads off into thick cover to
patrol one of the more densely
forested parts of her range.

LEFT Noon strides along the
lake shore on a regular tour of
her territory. She has killed and
eaten recently and her belly is
bulging.

Young males tend to spend their first independent years around the fringe areas of the forest transecting the ranges of one or more dominant males. But this movement outwards is temporary, and in a year or two they begin to move inwards in an attempt to usurp the resident dominant males and control important hunting grounds. The continuous process of assertion that occurs in Ranthambhore results in much shifting and adjusting. What is particularly interesting, however, is that the changes and shifts seem to occur during the monsoon, because soon afterwards, during the month of October, I have often found new animals have arrived. Let us look at the specific area of the three lakes.

Until October 1982 the area was occupied by two transient males; Padmini and her three nearly adult cubs; and two females, Nick Ear and Nasty. Laxmi was occasionally seen at the edges of the third lake with her three cubs. These tigers' territories overlapped for several months, but by the end of 1982 there were few signs of Padmini and her cubs except for the occasion (described later) when we encountered her controlling the feeding of eight other tigers over the carcass of a blue bull. From that time on she seemed to vanish, and so did her cubs. Padmini has now shifted her range to the far side of the forest near an area called Lahpur and no longer frequents her former range.

So, up to October/November 1982, about twelve tigers overlapped in the limited area of three to four square kilometres around the lakes. But from October 1982 to October 1983, most of our sightings were of Nick Ear, one other female, and the two transient males. Sightings of Nasty became infrequent by the middle of 1983, but Nick Ear focused her activity nearly every day around the area of the lakes.

From October 1983 onwards there was no further sign of Nick Ear and we realized that she had moved away from the lakes. Her activity was now behind the fort. A new resident female appeared, replacing Nick Ear, and we called her Noon. The two transient males also seemed to have left, and now a new male was strongly asserting his presence around the lakes. We named this male Genghis. Our first sightings of him were no more than fleeting glimpses as he seemed shy of human presence, but he gradually adjusted and spent a lot of time spray-marking, clawing, scraping the earth and vocalizing, all at such intense and regular levels that it seemed he was taking charge of the area. During this period a second female started using the area of the lakes and she seemed quite young. These were the three regular residents of the area. One transient female and one transient male also occasionally crossed this territory.

By October 1984 Genghis had moved out and the area of the lakes was frequented by another large male. He too was initially very elusive but slowly he adjusted, spending a lot of time marking and asserting his presence in the area. He seemed very different from Genghis in his general behaviour, though using the same paths, niches and water-holes. We called the new male Kublai. Let us for a moment examine Kublai's behaviour in 1984/5.

From late November to mid-December he spent nearly ten days vigorously asserting his presence in the area around the lakes. He then disappeared and was not seen again until 31 December. Our next sighting was on 3 February, in the evening, around Jogi Mahal. He had returned after a gap of 34 days. I was very excited to see him, perhaps because of the absence of Genghis and his own irregular presence. He sat by an ancient gate near Jogi Mahal and then moved round between the lakes. The next day we discovered that during the night he had eaten a chital doe, completely devouring it and leaving only bits and pieces of bone. He had already left before dawn when we went round to Rajbagh. He must have consumed 30 kilogrammes of meat in one sitting.

The next transient male tiger walked around the lakes on 25 February and then moved off towards Lakarda. On the evening of the same day Kublai was seen around Rajbagh again after an absence of 22 days. Kublai came again on 6 March and stayed around the lakes, with Noon, for about eight days.

I kept a detailed record of the month of March/April and from 16 March to 15 April, Kublai's pug marks were always somewhere in the vicinity of the lakes. He had begun to equal Genghis' record for that month. The sharp difference between the two was that Genghis indulged in much vocalization while taking over the area whereas Kublai seemed to have worked it out much more silently. They were, in fact, quite different personalities.

These tiger movements are extremely complex, and the reasons underlying them are very often far from clear. I know of one instance where a female wounded in a clash with another tiger moved twelve kilometres away from her area to a completely new spot near the resthouse. But why did Nick Ear leave when Genghis arrived? Why did Genghis leave and Kublai arrive? Had Kublai killed Genghis? These were difficult questions, apparently without any answers.

A tigress with very young cubs will initially have very localized movements which then shift and expand as the cubs grow. Maybe Nick Ear was with a litter, and her movement patterns had therefore changed. Situations of territory overlap between a male and several females have been seen in other areas of Ranthambhore, and I think that a male tiger will often accept females in his range although obviously there are exceptions to this, depending on the nature of the resident male. But it is also possible that even females may clash in an area with the more dominant ones driving the others to the fringes. Today it seems that the limited area of the lakes is a ground for much competition between males, who turn aggressive in a bid to retain their hold. Surprisingly Genghis, a prime male, seems to have relinquished his hold to another male with very little resistance.

The lakes support large concentrations of deer and therefore seem to be prime hunting grounds for the tiger. This factor may be responsible for the kind of changes that occur every year as new tigers take over from old ones.

From 15 October 1984 to 5 March 1985, Kublai's pug marks were seen on a total of 20 days in the area of the lakes. From 6 March to 15 April he spent 30 days there. Why is there such great variation in mobility?

I think it is related to the season. In March, most of the water-holes are drying up under the scorching sun and the area of the lakes receives a major influx of deer from nearby areas. This factor must force the tiger to follow suit, and therefore Kublai's concentration around the lakes was very similar to that of Genghis during the previous year. Differences in patterns of mobility can be startling. Genghis spent over six weeks in the summer of 1984 in the area of the three lakes, moving over only three or four square kilometres. At the same time, Akbar was covering 25-30 square kilometres. It would appear that in Akbar's range the prey were much more evenly and widely dispersed.

Mobility among tigers is an ever-changing phenomenon, affected by seasonal changes, prey movement and the availability of water. Tigers seem to be more mobile in the winter than the summer and this is probably due to the lower temperature and plentiful water which disperses the prey species around the numerous water-holes.

Do male tigers interact with other males in their area? I think that perhaps they do, but only rarely. I have only once seen two adult males strolling together and then stalking off in search of prey. I have also seen two male siblings clash just after breaking away from the family, but before becoming vicious one of the males submitted, rolling on his back twice, and peace descended. Males probably establish a rank order in an area, which is then accepted by all. Both George Schaller and Billy Arjan Singh record associations between resident and transient male tigers which were cordial. A.A.Dunbar Brander (1923) once observed three adult males hunting together. But Genghis never tolerated another male in the area for the year that he ruled around the lakes. Tigers seem very individualistic in their attitudes towards range and territory, and especially to the sharing of it.

THE LANGUAGE OF THE TIGER

Tigers have devised their own silent way of communicating their movements and establishing their territorial claims. This is done firstly by spray-marking. As the tiger, or tigress, walks along, it will turn its hindquarters

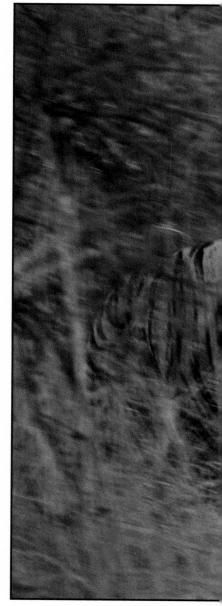

The dry deciduous forest of Ranthambhore provides an ideal background for this prowling tiger. His disruptive coat pattern of black, white and tan stripes breaks up the outline of his body and blends perfectly with the swaying grasses and the dry branches of trees and bushes.

towards a tree, bush, or patch of grass, and with a vertically-raised tail shoot out a spray of fluid, hitting the object at an upward angle. The fluid stream of the male is narrow compared with that of the female. The fluid smells musky and strong, and is a mixture of urine and a secretion from the anal glands. After ejecting this spray, I have on numerous occasions seen a tiger sniffing it and then hanging his tongue out with the nose wrinkled, a gesture referred to as 'flehmen'. Tigers will also indulge in flehmen when sniffing another tiger's scent on an object. The smell can last for up to 40 days and is an excellent indication to other tigers of how recently a tiger has passed by, and whether or not the area is 'occupied'. This may discourage other tigers – or encourage them – depending on the precise stituation.

Cubs can follow their mothers through their scent, and a tigress in oestrus will attract the male tiger by using it as a means of pin-pointing her location. Fresh scent can indicate a dangerous encounter, especially between males, whereas an old scent may be a signal that the animal can go ahead with care; but I have noticed that be it stale or fresh, the scent of another tiger will be sniffed at and resprayed by the passing tiger who thereby asserts his own claim to the spot.

Up until 1980 I had never seen a tiger spray-marking in Ranthambhore, and this was partly due to the fact that the tiger had not then shed its nocturnal habits, and partly because of the smaller population in the Park and the correspondingly low level of interaction between tigers. In the last four years it has become normal activity throughout the year, and especially after the rains.

Most tigers I have seen in Ranthambhore seem to prefer depositing their faeces on the central grass strip that runs down the middle of the road, or at the edge of the road on a patch of grass. They do not cover their faeces, but we have frequently observed scrape marks around the spot as if the soil and grass have been raked. Sometimes defecation has taken place, in other cases urination has occured, but at times the animal has simply left scrape marks. On five occasions I have seen just a tiny sample of defecation on a raked patch, as if marking the spot; obviously it is yet another way of communicating the tiger's presence to others.

Genghis, when he was new to the area of the three lakes, indulged in regular and incessant spray-marking, tree-clawing, soil-scraping, defecation and vocalization. This activity was intense in October and November of 1983, and lessened slightly as he established control. On one walk around the lakes he covered a distance of two kilometres in 75 minutes and spray-marked 18 trees, scraped the soil seven times, defecated once, and raked his claws on the bark of five trees. He also clutched the branches of two trees in his forepaws while standing on his rear legs.

Be it clawing, spraying or scratching, the intensity of this activity is concentrated on the animal paths, *nallahs* and man-made roads that criss-cross the forest in Ranthambhore. The reason for this is probably that such belts and paths act as natural boundaries, demarcating areas and ranges, especially for resident male tigers. Specific trees in such areas are regularly sprayed and clawed, more so when a new tiger is asserting his rights over an area. Kublai, for instance, indulged continuously in this activity through November and December but it eased off by March when his presence in the area was established. Genghis did much the same the year before.

Even more interesting as a form of communication is the range of sound made by the tiger. These animals are not very vocal by nature. They use sound far less frequently, for example, than do lions. So whenever I hear the roar of a tiger I feel a surge of excitement and anticipation because they never vocalize without a specific reason.

The most common sound is the roar; a resonant sound like 'aaoom'

BELOW RIGHT Kublai prepares to spray-mark the trunk of a tree at the edge of his territory – a remarkable photograph which clearly shows the male tiger's extraordinary ability to reverse the penis between the rear legs in order to shoot the jet of fluid onto the chosen tree, rock or clump of grass.

BELOW Pausing momentarily, Laxmi raises her tail and spray-marks a clump of grass at the side of the road. The strong-smelling fluid – a mixture of urine and a secretion from the anal glands – will linger for several weeks, proclaiming Laxmi's presence to any intruding tiger. Fateh spent many years patiently following tigresses in order to capture, on film, this second or two of territorial behaviour.

LEFT A tiger's immediate response, on catching the scent of another tiger's spray-mark, is to examine the area in detail — repeatedly sniffing the spot where the spray struck in order to assess the sex of the maker and the freshness of the mark.

which reverberates through the forest. During the latter part of 1983 and until the middle of 1984 Genghis spent many evenings roaring and on one occasion he roared 36 times in 84 minutes. On three occasions this was due to the presence of a tigress in close proximity and once he repeatedly answered the roar of another tiger a couple of kilometres away.

I remember 15 January 1984 vividly. I had just left the warmth of the fire to head for my sleeping bag, and was about to enter my room when the resounding roar of a tiger shattered the silence. It was so close that I was stunned. Barely 15 metres away a black shadow walked across Jogi Mahal, roaring continually. The sound continued for some 35 minutes as the tiger walked around Padam Talao. It had an almost paralysing power, and even after it had faded it seemed to reverberate in my mind. Sleep came slowly. The next morning we discovered that it was Genghis on his new beat.

The roar is a sound that echoes long distances and is used by a male tiger asserting his territorial right either by inviting another tiger to possible conflict or encouraging its hurried departure. Roaring is therefore a long-distance communication between tigers and it definitely has greater intensity and regularity when tigers are asserting themselves. Twice I have heard a tigress and on several occasions a male use this sound to respond to a cacophony of alarm calls from sambar, chital and langur who had spotted the threat. The tiger roared as if in annoyance and most of the alarms fell silent after that.

F.W. Champion captured some of the power of this sound in *With Camera in Tiger Land* (1927). He wrote, 'I remember an occasion when I was waiting on Balmati in a dense jungle just as night was closing in, listening to a roaring tiger coming closer and closer. When it was practically dark the animal came to within 20 yards of where we were waiting, by which time the volume and malignity of the roaring seemed simply appalling. The whole dark forest seemed to vibrate with the very sound and I confess that, accustomed as I am to the roaring of tigers, I began to feel somewhat nervous . . .'

On 20 January 1985, the large male tiger Akbar was found vocalizing with extraordinary frequency around the area of Malik Talao and Lakarda. His roar could be heard echoing out of a deep gorge. On 22 January, again following these sounds, he was located near the Lakarda water-hole. By 5.00 p.m. he had roared some ten times, and between 5.00 and 5.50 p.m. he must have vocalized 30 times more as he got ready to move and then slowly strode off. Besides the loud 'aaoom' sound he also emitted a 'oon' sound, like a half-note, while resting his head on his paws, and punctuated these calls with louder calls of 'aaoon' for which he lifted his head to open his

mouth. Throughout the day, Akbar appeared in a highly agitated state. He had several erections when lying on his back and he stretched himself frequently. He also licked his genitals a few times. I have not noted such behaviour in a prime male tiger before and I don't know the reason for this regular and intensive vocalization. Normally a tigress in oestrus will attract a male through this vocalization. Can male tigers suffer from periods of sexual frustration?

In *The Highlands of Central India* (1872), Captain J. Forsyth describes an unusual range of vocalization. 'I listened one night to the most remarkable serenade of tigers I ever heard. A peculiar long wail, like the drawn out mew of a huge cat first rose from a river course a few hundred yards below my tent. Presently, from a mile or so higher up the river, came a deep tremendous roar which had scarcely died away ere it was answered from behind my camp by another pitched in yet a deeper tone, startling us from its suddenness and proximity. All three were repeated at short intervals as the three tigers approached each other along the bottoms of the deep, dry water courses between and above which the camp had been pitched. As they drew together the noise ceased for about a quarter of an hour and I was dozing off to sleep again when suddenly arose the most fearful din near to where the tigress had first sounded the love note to her rival lovers, a din like the caterwauling of midnight cats magnified a hundred fold. Intervals of silence broken by the outburst of this infernal shrieking and moaning disturbed our rest for the next hour, dying away gradually as the tigers retreated along the bed of the river. In the morning I found all the incidents of a three volume novel in feline life imprinted on the sand, and marks of blood showed how genuine the combat part of the performance had been.'

There have been several occasions when following a female in oestrus I have heard her moan. This sound is subdued, at a lower pitch than a roar, and is used with great frequency by a tigress in oestrus. The sharp aggressive woof and cough of tigers I have only heard twice. First when two male tigers confronted each other in the forest, woofing and leaping and then woofing and coughing, face to face at a distance of a few centimetres. It is a very sharp and loud sound, and chilling for the listener. On the second occasion, just before and during the eating of a spotted deer, two adult females used much the same sound especially before adjusting to the process of eating during which they also snarled, growled and hissed. The sounds started off with great ferocity but after an hour they seemed to fade into a lower key.

F.W. Champion (1927) describes a similar situation. 'For the next hour they quarrelled violently over their meal, making the most awful growls and snarls as they demolished the carcass, while I, shaking with suppressed excitement, sat pondering upon my foolishness in having allowed my *machan* [tree platform] to be tied in such an insecure position. Every now and then there would be a terrific outburst of snarling as one of them drove the other away from the kill ...'

I have never heard tigers purring or miaowing, but then I have never encountered a tigress with very young cubs in Ranthambhore. Once from a distance I heard a miaowing coming from deep within a cave up a cliff, but I was unable to confirm the source. On three separate occasions while observing Padmini and her first and second litters I heard a bird-like sound, a 'pook' or a squeak, at which the cubs disappeared rapidly behind their mother. In similar situations with mothers and cubs I have heard a kind of soft grunt used very effectively by mothers in bringing their cubs to heel. It is not a sound you would normally associate with the tiger and appears to be a quiet way of communication so that the forest and its inhabitants are not unduly alarmed.

Growling and snarling are sounds I have heard on several occasions. Often a tigress annoyed at her semi-adult cubs has emitted a low growl that seems to come from deep within and seems to linger in the air. A sharp aggressive growl-cum-roar has been heard on several occasions when angry tigers have mock-charged my jeep, vocalizing loudly while leaping towards me. We have often been snarled at by tigers while observing them. Here the

LEFT Once a spray-mark has been examined, the tiger wrinkles its nose and allows its tongue to hang from its open mouth in the gesture known as 'flehmen'. The expression may be held for a full minute or more, after which the tiger will respray the spot and perhaps also rake his claws across it, thereby superimposing his own claim over it.

LEFT Tigers will also rake the bark of tree trunks and branches at strategic points on their territory – and particularly along roads, paths and junctions that mark the boundaries of their range. Here Kublai reaches up some 3.3m to claw a leaning branch. The tiger hung there for 30 seconds before dropping back onto all fours.

tiger holds its mouth slightly open, bares its canines, wrinkles its nose and exhales. On another occasion a low growling snarl was used by a male tiger that had seized the kill of a tigress. Any effort by her to join him was met with this sound, and over a couple of hours she was driven farther and farther away. Twice I have heard a strange blowing sound like a continuous puffing, made by a tiger that had settled down to eat after protecting a kill for several hours.

Aggressive interactions between tigers have been difficult to observe, and I can count on my fingers the times this has been possible. But very seldom do tigers end up in a fatal conflict; the tension invariably dissolves before any real harm can be done. Once, a month after Akbar had broken away from his family, I came upon Babar and Laxmi sitting behind a bush at the edge of the fort. As darkness descended on the forest I saw Babar and Laxmi become alert, and a few minutes later Akbar strolled down an incline towards them. Woofing and coughing, Babar and Akbar leapt towards each other in direct confrontation, standing nose to nose, coughing viciously and attempting a mock boxing fight. The forest resounded with the most blood-curdling sounds and then suddenly these died down altogether and I saw Babar adopt a posture of submission by rolling on his back twice with his forepaws raised upwards to the sky. Laxmi sat behind a bush watching the scene, and after Akbar had spent a few seconds looking at Babar on his back on the ground, he strolled off into the distance. Babar then joined Laxmi and they too moved off. It was quite an unusual interaction, with Akbar – assuming the role of the dominant tiger – asserting his territorial right over Babar, with whom he had grown up.

This incident happened in 1978. But in 1984 Fateh had the opportunity to see Akbar and Laxmi interacting. Following Akbar down the road, Fateh found him branching off into a stream bed and suddenly from the cover of a bush Laxmi appeared, striding out aggressively. Akbar coughed three times and immediately Laxmi rolled over on the ground, her legs upwards. Akbar watched for half a minute before continuing his journey. Again a situation of inherent aggression had been resolved by a submissive posture.

Aggression between tigers occurs most commonly around food and the process of feeding, especially when adult animals feed together. However, such situations are rare and the few occasions on which we have been lucky enough to observe them are detailed in the next chapter.

Not surprisingly there have been times when we, the observers, have attracted hostility. There was the time when the tigress Nasty became very aggressive towards human beings. This was during the first five months of 1983. Nasty charged us 17 times during these months – and not always when we could see her!

I remember one occasion when a burst of alarm calls had me moving rapidly towards the sound. I switched off the engine near a patch of tall grass and scanned the landscape, listening intently. Sambar and chital alarm calls echoed around Rajbagh and the monkeys were chattering incessantly on a tree. Suddenly I heard the grass rustling on my right and had a momentary glimpse of Nasty charging the jeep. I immediately started the engine and put the jeep into reverse gear. She stopped, snarling, tail twitching and ears held back, and I sat some 100 metres away watching. Then for no reason she charged again and chased me for another 100 metres after which I decided to leave the area, almost paralysed by the shock of the charge. I still have not fathomed the reason for her aggression. Annoyance at a jeep? Her period of oestrus? An injury? Or just a moment of anger? It could have been anything. But her aggression ended during the middle of 1983 and she never charged us again. Genghis once charged our jeep, ending up only a metre or so away and I thought for a moment he might take over the wheel. But these charges were threats and never culminated in an actual attack.

This mock charging has, on a few occasions, been directed at the trackers on their bicycles. Twice a tigress charged them from the cover of tall grass, vocalizing loudly. Once she slapped the wheel of the bicycle and both tracker and cycle fell to the ground. On both occasions the tigress was feeding in the grass, unknown to the tracker.

One of the most awe-inspiring sights in nature: a prime male tiger displaying outright aggression. Genghis, angered for some reason, snarls viciously at us, baring his huge canines and exhaling with a blood-chilling low-pitched hiss. In the course of our studies we have had to face several mock charges, but usually aggression takes the form of a threat display only. Between tigers, physical attack is usually prevented by one or other animal backing down with a gesture of submission.

NON-FAMILY ASSOCIATIONS

Tigers have always been regarded as solitary animals but in 1983 two adult groups were very active between Malik Talao and Lakarda. In the first there were two males, one larger than the other, and three females. Except for one of the males, it was very difficult to distinguish the animals by size. They could even have been a family that never split up. Their general behaviour when hunting was not unlike a pride of lions. Around the meadows of the third lake they would take five different positions and lie in wait. If a deer came into the circle, one tiger would first stalk and then go for it, pushing it towards one of the others, and in this way they would confuse the deer as they swept through the meadow.

From the summer of 1983 to early 1984 another adult group of tigers roamed between Malik Talao and Lakarda and Kachida. This also comprised two males and three females. Most of our observations of this group were in relation to hunting. One female was the dominant member of the group and seemed to control its movements. But in February 1984 this group changed and I found one male with two females. One month later, I found one male

with one female and discovered the second female with a gash on her rear flank, presumably the result of a conflict within the group.

In both groups it appears that the tigers remained together for varying periods of time and that the numbers within the group underwent considerable change due to conflict which may have been caused by a tigress coming into oestrus or by aggressive squabbles over food. Past observations of similar adult groups are quite illuminating.

In *Wild Animals in Central India* (1927), A.A. Dunbar Brander states, 'The largest party I have even seen together consisted of six animals; one large male and two fully grown females accompanied by three young animals almost as big as the tigers.'

Edward B. Baker in his book *Sport in Bengal* (1886), writes that, 'This animal is not the unsociable creature it is commonly understood to be. On the contrary, it is fond of consorting with others, and not seldom three or four may be found together; a mother and nearly full grown cubs; both parents and half grown ones, or a charming party of young males and females living and hunting together for a considerable length of time.'

I describe below a typical day in my own observations of an adult group in Ranthambhore. It is January 1984; eight o'clock in the morning. I am driving down the Kachida valley and it is icy cold. Suddenly I spot three adult tigers sitting in a clearing at the edge of the road; an adult male, accompanied by two adult females. They soon get up, the male pausing briefly for some water in the *nallah*, and move off into slightly thicker forest to rest. They sit at distances of ten to twelve metres from each other.

An hour passes. With some difficulty I can see the stripes of one of the tigers. There is no movement until 12.10 p.m. as all three tigers sleep. Then one of the females gets up and is followed by the second female. The second female pauses for a moment to rake the trunk of a tree with her forepaws, and then moves on. The male now follows. They walk some 100 metres before coming to a pool of water and each one proceeds to drink, but separately, two sitting nearby as the third drinks. The female who is leading them seems dominant and she nuzzles the male before going to sleep in the shade of a tree. The other two do the same.

After nearly an hour of sleeping and lazing, the dominant female gets up and starts to walk away, followed slowly by the second female and then the male. The two females walk on one side of the stream bed and the male on the other. The time is 1.40 p.m. Occasionally sitting, spraying, clawing and on one occasion even jumping on to the low-lying branch of a tree, all three tigers proceed leisurely, covering about two-and-a-half kilometres in two

RIGHT Aggression between tigers does sometimes spill over into physical violence, as demonstrated by the huge tear in the flank of this young tigress. She was a member of an adult group that roamed the forest for some months, and probably suffered the injury during a clash over food. The tigress left the group and moved some 14km away. Hampered by the wound she was unable to hunt efficiently and so lost weight rapidly. But slowly she recovered. She constantly licked the wound with her rough tongue, keeping it free of dirt and enabling her antiseptic saliva to do its work.

LEFT 'Pride' behaviour is unusual in tigers but non-family groups have occasionally been seen in Ranthambhore, including this group which roamed the Kachida valley together for about seven months. The reasons for such associations could be related to improved hunting efficiency but much more research is needed before we can draw any firm conclusions about them.

hours. I see no signs of deer but on nearing a water-hole four sambar are visible, feeding on the grass. The two females who are walking one behind the other go into a crouch and in slow motion start moving towards the sambar. This is a typical stalk and not a sound can be heard as the tiger's soft pads move over the ground. The male tiger moves in from the other side in an attempt to cut off the sambar. But all is in vain as the sambar soon move off toward a salt lick. But the tigers follow at varying distances and from different angles. Their crouched postures and stalking continues over a further 100 metres, with brief intervals of a faster loping gait when the cover thickens. There are still no alarms from the deer.

Farther on I see an opening in the forest where some eight sambar have congregated around a natural salt lick. I position myself and wait. After ten minutes of silence, with no alarms, the peace is shattered as the two females from one direction and the male from the other rush at full speed into the clearing. Amidst the booming alarm of the sambar I see them escape the tigers' rush by centimetres; just evading the jaws of death in the tigers' pincer movement. Soon the forest echoes with the sounds of alarm from sambar and langur monkeys and this discordant sound is interspersed with three low roars from a tiger. The three tigers then proceed to lie in the thick of the forest. I leave at dusk, thinking about the tigers' hunting prowess, and wondering at the complexity of the relationships between hunters and hunted.

THE HUNTED
AND THE HUNTERS

The morning of 5 January 1985 dawns cold and misty as we drive down towards Malik Talao. A group of chital and a few sambar are grazing in the grassy meadow behind the lake. Some 20 metres away a tigress is concealed in a patch of tall grass. She sits absolutely motionless, watching the movements of the deer. Occasionally a chital strays a few metres towards her and she cocks her head up and watches alertly. At one point she rises on her haunches and peers carefully over the grass, checking her position in relation to the deer.

She settles again, quite still. Unaware of danger, a sambar moves some five metres towards her. The tigress lifts her head, a quiver runs through her body, and then in a kind of slow motion she stalks forward with her belly touching the ground. She moves a couple of metres. The sambar looks up suspiciously and the tigress drops her head down, completely concealed in the cover of the high grass. The sambar is only ten metres away but the tigress makes no attempt to rush. A crested hawk eagle flies overhead. A couple of partridges scuttle away into a bush. A peacock cries in alarm. Soon the sambar drifts away and the chital move off. The tigress lifts her head for a moment, surveying the situation. She then proceeds to sleep in that position, her ears ever alert and responsive to sound. It is 9.30 a.m. She has not been spotted by the deer. She stays in the same patch of grass all day, waiting for the deer to drift close enough for her to launch her attack over a short distance.

In Ranthambhore the hunting techniques of tigers vary tremendously depending on the individual and its mood at the time. In general the tigers tend to spend a fair amount of time walking their beats, and this mainly on man-made roads, animal paths or along stream beds. In the process of doing this they cover areas where deer graze, congregate, or are moving from one point to another. When the eyes or ears of a tiger pick up any indication of prey, the animal tends first to freeze, then to crouch and then to start a careful, silent, slow-motion movement towards its prey.

The second common method is to take up a position near a water-hole or grassy meadow and remain concealed until the unsuspecting deer move in closer. I have found that this activity is more prevalent during the summer when the deer are forced towards water in large numbers, and a tiger will rarely move from its concealed spot for the whole day, especially if it remains undetected.

The bulk of this chapter is devoted to the tiger's six principal prey species in Ranthambhore; the sambar, chital, wild boar, nilgai, langur and peafowl. For each in turn a brief review of the animal's characteristics, feeding habits, breeding behaviour and movements within the forest will provide a background against which to view the hunting techniques employed against it by the tiger.

A sambar hind stares intently towards a thicket of long grass – alert, suspicious, but unable to see the perfectly camouflaged form of the tigress Noon. The sambar is a large, swift-footed animal and even at this range the hind is safe. To have any chance of making a kill, Noon will have to use all her stealth and patience, closing the gap a few centimetres at a time until she is close enough to make her final rush.

THE SAMBAR

The sambar is the most important prey species of the tiger in Ranthambhore and its numbers in the reserve probably exceed 4,000. It is the largest of the

Sambar and chital graze peacefully in and around the waters of Rajbagh. January is the height of the rutting season for the sambar, and much of their courtship and mating behaviour can be observed from the cover of the forest.

Indian deer and a fully grown stag can weigh between 225 and 320 kilogrammes. The adult male is dark brown in colour but the females are paler. The stags have a ruff of hair around the neck and throat and their coats are coarse. The height at the shoulder is up to 1.5 metres. The sambar is remarkably adaptable. It is found in the Himalayan foothills at heights of over 3,000 metres, in the evergreen and semi-evergreen forests across India, and in the dry deciduous and moist deciduous forests and thorn forests of Gujarat and Rajasthan.

Observers like Brander and Kesri Singh felt that the sambar was mainly nocturnal in habit, retreating into heavy cover during the day. Colonel Kesri Singh early this century found it difficult even to find a sambar in Ranthambhore, and records a full day in its search without even seeing, 'the tip of its tail'. Today the sambar is completely diurnal in Ranthambhore and no day can pass without it being seen; a fact no doubt related to the lack of disturbance in the Park. The sambar's diet consists mainly of leaves and grass combined with a wide assortment of wild fruit. Both stag and hind will feed on leaves and fruits by standing on their hind legs and plucking them off the branches. Sometimes a stag will break low branches with his antlers in order to eat the leaves.

With the advent of summer, sambar concentrations are high throughout the forest. Even in the drier areas it is quite possible to find 40 to 50 animals together, while very much larger congregations are found around the lakes, where they readily take to the water. They remain partly submerged for long periods, eating the weeds, lotus leaves and other water plants. Sometimes nearly 100 deer can be seen, heads bobbing up and down, a sight unique to Ranthambhore. January is referred to as their 'rutting period' and is the month when courtship and mating is at its peak.

On 29 January I found some 85 sambar in the water. Several egrets and pond herons kept them company, settling on their backs and fishing around their legs. Two dominant stags seemed to have monopolized two large

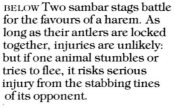

BELOW Two sambar stags battle for the favours of a harem. As long as their antlers are locked together, injuries are unlikely: but if one animal stumbles or tries to flee, it risks serious injury from the stabbing tines of its opponent.

groups of hinds, and several younger stags were waiting on the sidelines for their opportunity to court a hind. Then a third stag entered the water and moved towards one of the dominant males. Quickly they circled each other, and then they fought, with their heads lowered and their antlers locked together – pushing and straining at each other with all their might. It was a trial of strength in a bid to associate with the hinds, but the stag that had first entered the fray gave way amidst much splashing, and retired. The victor moved back to his harem. Sometimes these fights can be quite vicious and it is not uncommon to find battle-scarred stags with bloody wounds. I have even seen antlers break off in such fights.

Nearby, three pairs of young stags are sparring in the water amidst much grunting and squeaking. At the edge of the lake, in front of me, the sambar have made a wallow-hole and a young stag moves to it from the water. He stands in this muddy wallow and first dips his head down, spraying a stream of urine into the hole. He then flops into the mud and rolls several times on his back with all four legs in the air. He is joined at the wallow by a small sambar fawn who sniffs the stag and then walks around the hole. After several vigorous rolls the stag stands up, his brown coat glistening with a film of wet mud. He moves off to some tall grass and thrashes his antlers in it, and then moves on to a tree where he rubs his antlers up and down the bark, completely engrossed in this hectic activity. He now looks a frightful mess, his eyes straining and his coat wet, filthy and caked in mud. This behaviour is typical of a rutting stag and will continue until the end of February when the courting season eases off. The stag now walks back into the water, his eyes glazed and the glands below them swollen.

Suddenly I notice one of the dominant stags in the water sniffing and licking a female. He follows her for several paces, emitting a low grunting sound. She stops, raises her tail and the adult male mounts her in an attempt to copulate. A young male approaches the courting couple but is chased away by the dominant stag who rears up on his hind legs and kicks

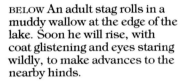

BELOW An adult stag rolls in a muddy wallow at the edge of the lake. Soon he will rise, with coat glistening and eyes staring wildly, to make advances to the nearby hinds.

RIGHT Having chased competing stags out of the immediate vicinity, a mature sambar stag mounts a hind in the shallow waters of Rajbagh. He has been thrashing his antlers in the lakeside vegetation and strands of grass and weed still cling to the tines.

the intruder away. Sambar do this occasionally and I have even seen hinds in the water rising up to fight with each other, kicking outwards with their forelegs. Both the dominant stags seem to have harems of ten to fourteen hinds and each has an audience of young males and fawns, the latter tending to keep to the shore, out of the way. The sun sets and I depart, leaving the sambars frolicking in the water.

In March the adult stags resume their solitary life until the next season. April, May and June are when the antlers are shed, but they soon start to grow back and remain 'in velvet' during the monsoon, clearing and hardening by the end of October. The velvet is basically a soft kind of skin. It has a rich blood supply and nourishes the growing antlers until they attain their full size, often more than a metre in length. The velvet is sensitive and vulnerable and the deer take great care to avoid any injury to it while the antlers are growing. Once the antlers have finished growing, the velvet is rubbed off against trees and bushes.

The gestation period of the sambar is about seven to eight months, and hours after its birth the young fawn is able to follow the mother easily and even run flat out if necessary. Most of the young are born during September, October and November with a few even later. The mother has a close relationship with her young until they attain maturity, suckling, licking and cleaning them regularly.

Leadership of the group is normally assumed by a hind, and she is seldom challenged. The leader is always the most alert and cautious, warning the group of any danger. Even when adult males associate with the group, the leadership is left to the hind. When she moves, the entire group will follow, in single file – a sight I have witnessed on several occasions.

Sambar have good eye-sight and can pick out moving objects at some distance, but it is to sound and smell that they are most sensitive. When a sambar senses danger the hairs around its neck and back bristle, it will flick its tail into a vertical position and stamp its forefoot in alarm. All indications point in the direction of the danger. Head up, it will sniff the air and if the suspicion is confirmed the sambar emits its loud, booming alarm call which can resound sometimes for nearly a kilometre and serves as a warning to the whole area. A mother with a fawn will also give a few alarm calls if she spots a jackal or hyena as the young fawn is extremely vulnerable to attacks by these predators. Sometimes suspicions are raised by movements in the grass, and on one occasion I heard hinds call in alarm when a jungle cat was walking nearby. Today, because of the high level of predation, they are extremely sensitive and on a windy day they call at the slightest sound, sometimes even at a chital who enters or exits from the grass.

The adult sambar is known to be very aggressive towards the leopard and I have never seen any evidence of a sambar being killed by this animal. However, one of our trackers recorded an exciting interaction between the two in Ranthambhore. A large male leopard was strolling by the edge of a stream one evening when suddenly it climbed into a tree and hid itself in the lower branches. Around the corner came three sambar hinds, which proceeded to drink some water right below the tree. The leopard leapt on to one and they both went crashing into the water. After much splashing and struggling the hind managed to escape leaving behind a rather surprised and very wet leopard.

Another predator especially of sambar fawns is the crocodile, which abounds in the waters of the first three lakes. On several occasions I have witnessed aggressive interactions in the water between an adult sambar and a crocodile but most of the time the former will, with a lot of splashing and kicking, beat off the attack. In fact, adult sambars and crocodiles co-exist relatively peacefully within the waters of the lake. The young fawns, however, sometimes follow their mothers into deep water and fall victim to a crocodile. There are a few eye-witness accounts of such happenings but my first clear sighting of this occurred at noon on 14 Janurary 1985. At the edge of one of the corners of Rajbagh I spotted a small brown body lying near a crocodile. On examining it through binoculars it turned out to be the carcass of a sambar fawn. I moved in closer to discover that the crocodile was

BELOW Younger stags and unreceptive hinds graze quietly in the lake some distance away from the hectic activities of the dominant males. An egret is just about to land on the back of one of the hinds.

Four adult sambar stags graze at sunset in Rajbagh lake. Two have lost parts of their antlers in the constant battles for supremacy that attend the mating season. But the antlers have served their purpose; they will soon be shed and a fresh set will grow in readiness for the next mating season.

LEFT Indian marsh crocodiles lurking amongst the dense mats of water-plants pose a constant threat to young sambar fawns venturing into the shallows of Rajbagh to drink. The crocodile will spend a long time on the shore with the fawn firmly grasped in its jaws, waiting for the carcass to putrefy. Its teeth are too blunt to tear the hide of a freshly killed animal.

grasping in its jaws the uneaten carcass of the fawn. Fifteen mintues later some sambar hinds moving towards the water stopped sharply on sighting the crocodile. One of them looked directly at the crocodile, raising its forefoot and flicking its tail. Very gradually they all moved towards the water, and after 30 minutes the crocodile decided to glide back into the deeper water, dragging the fawn with it. The fawn must have been freshly killed as the carcass did not float.

Later that afternoon the crocodile was back on the shore with the sambar, gripping the head firmly in its jaws. It still had not been able to eat. It sat out in the sun for 35 minutes before retreating with its kill into the water. I found no signs of it late in the evening, or the next day. It appears that the crocodile only eats after an animal is putrefied, as only then is it able to open the carcass with ease.

The tiger, of course, is the most important predator of sambar in Ranthambhore, though I have rarely found kills of adult stags. The sambar is large and heavy, but can take off rapidly when necessary. Only mature and experienced tigers can kill successfully. I remember following the tigress Nick Ear at 7.00 a.m. one morning in November 1982, as she strolled along a road with the backdrop of the fort behind her. A troop of monkeys were barking in alarm. Nick Ear sprayed two bushes and then moved into a patch of grass, flushing out a sambar who rapidly disappeared into thicker forest, calling loudly. Nick Ear moved back onto the road, stopping by a patch of water to drink before walking on.

On her way she spotted a group of peacocks and leapt after them, but unsuccessfully. A pair of lapwings shrieked in alarm around her. She continued walking for half a kilometre until she came to a bush some 15 metres from a water-hole. She vanished into the bush and went to sleep. Just after 2.30 p.m. a large sambar stag cautiously approached the water-hole. Suddenly I felt my heart pounding, realizing the proximity of the sambar to the tigress. The deer swerved slightly, moving right up to the bush that concealed Nick Ear. I watched, paralysed. As the sambar passed the bush, the tigress leapt out, clumsily, and a stunned sambar wheeled around, jumping backwards and then calling in alarm. Sambar and tigress watched each other for a few seconds before the sambar turned and dashed away, calling loudly on the way. The tigress had missed at a distance of less than two metres; she had taken a few seconds too long in coming out of the bush, and had lost her chance.

The sambar have a great penchant for water, and since they enjoy moving into the lakes to feed there are always large congregations around the first three lakes, which are surrounded by high grass through which the sambar enter and exit. At the onset of the summer this movement continues throughout the day.

In April 1983, before Genghis came into our lives, Nick Ear gave us an astonishing performance. At 3.00 p.m. we found her concealed in a bank of grass, carefully watching some sambar about 50 metres away in the water. Shortly afterwards she came right out into the open and in slow motion covered the 45 metres to the edge of the water one step at a time, freezing every time the sambar glanced upwards. This confrontation between predator and prey was hypnotic. Just as Nick Ear reached the water's edge, one of the sambar hinds saw her and bellowed in alarm, and Nick Ear charged into the water, splashing and wading through it with powerful strides and then breaking into a swim. The sambar she was chasing escaped out of the water, bellowing continuously. She repeated this charge again the next day at the same time, but again unsuccessfully. I think she was exploring the hunting technique that Genghis was to exploit so successfully a year later. Her careful stalk in the open, which alternated between motion and freezing, was unique – and the sambar remained undisturbed until she reached the lakeside. Only her lack of skill in attacking in water prevented her success.

Colonel Kesri Singh describes a remarkable evening observing a tiger on a sambar carcass in the forest of Ranthambhore during the first part of this

BELOW Crocodiles pose no real threat to adult sambar hinds heading towards the lake to feed and drink. The tree-pie, one of Ranthambhore's most common birds, feeds on the ticks and other insects living in the sambar's coat and on its skin.

LEFT Noon drags a freshly killed sambar hind into a dense thicket at the edge of the lake.

century. On receiving news that a tiger had killed a large sambar he went off and observed the tiger eating for nearly 30 minutes. Suddenly the tiger looked up. In the distance the cries of wild dogs echoed and their sounds seemed to be approaching. The tiger appeared anxious and uncomfortable but remained with his kill. Soon the wild dogs arrived and surrounded the tiger, inching closer with loud cries. The tiger growled back viciously and the dogs whimpered. The tiger then rushed at them, striking a couple with its paws, but then decided to flee through the opening it had made in the circle. The tiger's kill had been appropriated. He disappeared from sight and the dogs tore at the carcass. This is truly a unique description, because today the wild dog, or dhole, is no longer found in Ranthambhore.

We have had ten sightings of tigers feeding on sambar. On most of these occasions, intervening vegetation has prevented clear vision, but of all these situations the most interesting occurred with Laxmi, in early March 1984, on the Kachida road. Our three-day observation of Laxmi feeding, and her interaction with the male tiger Broken Tooth over the kill, is told in detail in the captions to the accompanying photo-essay.

In March 1984 a stroke of luck led us to a recent tiger kill near the Kachida valley, and over a period of three days we were able to watch a complex interaction, over the kill, between Laxmi and the male tiger Broken Tooth.

BELOW LEFT Day 1: 1.30 p.m. I am driving down a track leading into the Kachida Valley. Something is bothering me, and for no reason other than an instinctive feeling I take the jeep off the track and across country. In the distance a group of tree-pies attracts my attention and I set off to investigate. Not for the first time my instinct is rewarded; in a bend of a rocky stream bed I find Laxmi with a recently killed sambar hind.

ABOVE RIGHT Day 1: 2.00 p.m. Laxmi rolls onto her back, totally relaxed, having eaten a small part of the sambar's rump -- the choicest part and nearly always the first part of the carcass eaten by a tiger. Twice while dozing she is disturbed by thieving tree-pies which she drives off with snarls and a couple of mock charges.

RIGHT Day 1: 3.20 p.m. Laxmi rises, sniffs the carcass then paces round it. Catching it by the neck she attempts to move it, but then instead tries to cover it by scraping leaves and stones over it with her feet. Tigers tend to do this instinctively. I have never seen it done well enough to cover a carcass but the action probably does help to hide the meat from crows, tree-pies and vultures.

BELOW Day 1: 5.40 p.m. Laxmi feeds again, this time opening up part of the abdomen and devouring the sambar's intestines. After eating she settles down again to rest. A solitary Egyptian vulture flies slowly overhead, but like the tree-pies he will get nothing; Laxmi dozes, lying almost on top of her prey.

RIGHT Day 2: 6.35 a.m. On returning the next morning we are amazed to find a large male tiger sitting over the kill. Laxmi is 20m away, looking towards him. The new arrival is Broken Tooth, a resident of the Kachida valley. One of his lower canines is broken but otherwise he is a prime male. The sambar carcass has been greatly reduced. It is obvious that both tigers have feasted.

Day 2: 7.00 a.m. Laxmi looks towards the carcass, but each time she does so a soft warning snarl from Broken Tooth discourages her. He has appropriated her kill. Perhaps there had been some aggressive vocalization from Laxmi initially, but now she lies submissively at a distance.

Day 2: 8.45 a.m. After a short sleep, Laxmi rises and moves away. Broken Tooth lies with his head resting on the carcass: tigers appear to like being physically 'in touch' with their food. Between now and 11.00 a.m. Broken Tooth dozes – but five or six times he is disturbed by tree-pies trying to scavenge scraps of the kill.

Day 2: 3.00 p.m. It is now very hot and Broken Tooth rises, tugs at the sambar carcass, then lets go again. He turns and walks off towards a small water-hole. The temperature is nearly 40°C and in that heat quenching the thirst and soaking the body are essential activities for a tiger.

Day 2: 3.10 p.m. Broken Tooth returns, dripping and refreshed. He drags the carcass a short distance and settles down to eat. Soon we hear the incredible 'sawing' sound of his canines slicing through the sambar's hide, followed by the crunching of bone.

Day 2: 4.00 p.m. There is still no sign of Laxmi returning. Broken Tooth has spent the afternoon dozing and occasionally chewing on one of the sambar's hind legs. He settles down to sleep and we head back to the resthouse.

Day 3: 6.45 a.m. On our return to the stream bed we find Broken Tooth still 'in residence'. The sambar is almost eaten. Only the head, forelegs and part of the rib-cage remain. The tiger's belly is full and he looks much bigger. He sprawls beside the remains, a picture of contentment.

Day 3: 10.00 a.m. Broken Tooth is roused from his doze by the appearance of another female. She is carrying a wound in her rear flank and is obviously hungry. Broken Tooth snarls viciously, and the tigress retreats out of sight.

Day 3: 4.00 p.m. Broken Tooth strolls down to the water-hole and soaks himself, staying there for nearly 30 minutes. We decide to leave. About 2km along the track we come across Laxmi, sitting beside another *nallah*. I find myself wondering – is she planning the strategy for her next hunt, or thinking of the fine deer that was snatched from her by the big male tiger?

BELOW Noon feeds on the head of a sambar; all that remains of her last kill. Like most tigers she will waste nothing. When the meat is chewed off she will rasp the skull with her rough tongue until it is perfectly clean. Tigers have individual preferences when it comes to feeding. Many will eat the rumen and intestines of their prey, and some will eat meat even when it is rotten and infested with flies.

Nine times out of ten, tigers will finish every scrap of meat on an animal kill. Sometimes even the flesh around the skull is chewed. Very rarely is a kill deserted. I remember that nine years ago, when tigers in Ranthambhore were still fearful of men, a kill was immediately deserted at our approach. But today the tigers eat with observers looking on, and also consume every morsel, even if it means sitting out for three days or more. We have also noted that there is little desire to share. Some animals will share their food, but not the male tiger, who is very possessive, at any rate in Ranthambhore, and wastes very little meat. The scavenging birds have a hard time finding scraps. Once, in April 1984, I discovered Laxmi feeding on a sambar in a gorge. But she was doing a strange thing, removing the hair from the sambar's body. Starting from the neck she worked her way down the back, plucking out tufts of hair and spitting them out. It is the only time I have seen this.

THE CHITAL

March 1982. It is 8.30 a.m. and I have just returned from a morning drive. I decide to sit out on the balcony of Jogi Mahal and have a cup of hot coffee. I watch a crocodile as it glides through the water. A pied kingfisher hovers before dropping into the water like a stone, coming up again, seconds later, with a fish. The lotus flowers are about to bloom, and most of the lake is covered with a spread of green leaves. The morning drive has been uneventful and I wonder what the evening holds in store. My gaze drifts to a group of 14 chital grazing on the lush green grass at the edge of the lake. The coffee arrives and I take my first sip watching this serene lake and its surroundings when quite unexpectedly a cacophony of chital alarm calls diverts my attention to a tiger that has charged the herd from the tall grass, startling them into confusion and successfully catching one.

BELOW A herd of chital, or axis deer, grazing near one of the lakes. The animals are very nervous and very fast on their feet, yet they form a major part of the tiger's diet and are the second most important prey species in Ranthambhore.

LEFT Chital gather to feed on ber fruits dropped to the ground by langurs gorging themselves in the crown of the tree. The two species have an interdependent relationship in Ranthambhore — each providing the other with an extra level of security against surprise attack by predators.

The suddenness of the attack has caught me by surprise. The next moment, the tiger grips the neck of the chital and carries it off into the high grass around the lake. It looks as if it might be a doe. The whole event has lasted just two minutes and the lake is already back to its former serenity. I go off to investigate, and find that the kill was indeed a doe, now hidden in the grass thicket along with the indistinct shape of a tiger.

The chital is thought to have been present in India during the Pleistocene Period and is the most primitive of the true cervids. They are found commonly in most parts of India, especially in dry deciduous and moist deciduous forests. The dry forests of Ranthambhore have some 3,800 chital concentrated in areas near water, shade and grass, but I have never known them to enter the water like the sambar. An adult stag stands nearly a metre at the shoulder and can weigh 90 kilogrammes. The coat of the chital is a bright rufous fawn profusely spotted with white, although old stags are darker in colour. The graceful antlers have three tines, a long brow tine set nearly at right-angles to the beam and two branch tines at the top.

Chital are prolific eaters of leaves, shoots, and fruits. In Ranthambhore they have an interdependent relationship with the langur and can be seen gathered in much larger numbers than the sambar under the fruit trees on which the langurs feed. The chital seems to gain much more than the monkey from this relationship as the leaf litter and fallen fruit are provided almost entirely by the langurs. The other main benefit seems to stem from the fact that the association brings together many more eyes and ears to warn of approaching danger.

This is also the best situation in which to observe chital behaviour. I remember watching a herd below a troop of langurs on 6 March at 7.00 a.m. The langurs were busy eating and jumping from branch to branch of a spreading ber tree, the leaves and fruit of which were piled up below. A large dominant stag seemed to have claimed the prime position below the tree. A younger stag approached, but was quickly chased away. A doe feeding below

BELOW A chital stag basks in the early morning sun, the light reflecting off his velvet-covered antlers.

PREVIOUS PAGES Chital are invariably nervous when forced to pass close to an area of tall grass. The slightest movement or sound will create instant panic and the deer will flee — leaping and bounding away until they are well clear of the 'danger' area.

nipped another on her flank, and then both reared up on their hind legs, kicking their forelegs at each other, balancing precariously. There is much conflict below these trees; a continuous assertion of dominance. The stag then balanced on his hind legs and nibbled at the ber fruit on a low branch, repeating this action several times.

In the distance the forest echoes with the haunting ringing call of an adult stag. February, March and April seem to be the most active rutting period for the chital in Ranthambhore, though it continues sporadically all the year round. Another large stag comes towards the tree and now the two adults circle each other with heads held high and their ears at a peculiar angle. Then they stop, and with great force crash their antlers together. The conflict has carried the stags some six or seven metres away, their antlers entwined. They crash once more but now the loser is weary and is quickly chased away. Two other younger, immature, males are sparring some 20 metres away but this activity is more playful; a way of testing their strength.

The adult stag now sniffs at an oestrus doe who is sitting in the shade. He licks her face and attempts to nudge her side in an effort to make her stand.

She does, and he continues licking her. They move a few steps behind a thick bush where he mounts her and copulates. I have only seen chital mating twice before. The period of coitus is short and the dominant stag will copulate regularly with oestrus does in his harem. When does are unreceptive to his advances the stag sometimes charges them repeatedly until they submit. The stag now comes back into the open emitting a strange low growl, and follows it up with his repetitive hoarse rutting call. He then, much like the sambar, thrashes his antlers against a bush, pawing the ground repeatedly in a forceful display, and possibly also secreting a scent, thus asserting his supremacy over the other stags. Such a dominant one prefers to keep all other stags at a distance and will not tolerate intrusions. Stags with a large spread of antlers seem more confident and assertive and during the rut they strut around in a display of power. Be it sambar or chital, these antlers are a formidable defensive weapon against attacks by predators.

The gestation period is about seven months and chitals are successful breeders. Normally one fawn is dropped but I have occasionally come across twins. They are born at most times of the year, the intensity varying according to habitat and food availability. On 7 February 1983 I observed a newly dropped fawn and its mother away from the main herd, under the shade of a tree. The fawn must have arrived a short while before as the mother was vigorously licking it while the fawn attempted to balance itself on its feet, stumbling around and frantically searching for milk. The placenta was still oozing out of the mother and after it fell she immediately proceeded to eat it. In the meantime the fawn kept circling its mother, and after about 25 minutes discovered the teat and the milk. Soon after, that magical transformation took place providing strength and energy to the vulnerable and knock-kneed fawn who began to balance properly on all four feet and in another 30 minutes was following the mother quite briskly.

The mother, protective as ever, has to be constantly watchful of scavengers like the jackal which will pounce in a flash on the helpless fawn. I once witnessed a jackal carrying a tiny fawn away in its mouth. Another time I saw a chital doe with twins who must have been a few weeks old. A jungle cat suddenly appeared and proceeded to stalk towards a bush near the fawns. The doe spotted the cat and, tail raised, foot stamping, she walked towards the bush, forcing it away. Her twins were in the meantime squeaking in alarm.

Antlers are shed annually, usually after the rut, but stags carrying antlers in various stages of development have been seen in all seasons. Until the antlers attain their full length they are covered with velvet, much like those of the sambar and other deer. In Ranthambhore the chital do not cover long distances. They tend to remain in limited areas, moving back and forth a few kilometres. At the height of the summer they congregate in large numbers. Stag parties are quite common during September to January where ten to fifteen chital stags, some in velvet, will often be found roaming together.

In most cases an adult doe will act as leader of a chital group. I have seen a chital doe suddenly stop, sniff the air, raise her neck and, forefoot stamping, approach the direction of the supposed threat. The rest of the herd stands frozen, watching the leader. A few may even turn away. If the leader feels that there is danger, a sharp, shrill alarm call will ring out. Their suspicions are easily aroused, even in response to peacock alarms.

We had a startling afternoon with Nick Ear in the summer of 1983. Alerted by the cackle-barking of monkeys I found Nick Ear sitting on the wall of an abandoned well, shaded by a large tree. She nibbled at the branches as she lay on the wall, half dozing, half alert. At about 2.15 p.m. she changed her position by moving to the edge. Seconds later she was fully alert, freezing for a while in a deep crouch. Some distance away, three chital does were walking by. As they crossed some ten metres from the wall, Nick Ear leapt straight towards them. But it was to no avail: the chital bounded away. Surprisingly they did not bark in alarm even once; perhaps in such emergencies all the animals' energies are so concentrated in fleeing that vocalization is simply not possible.

Nick Ear then went and sat in a grassy patch above a stream bed. An hour

BELOW Noon breaks cover and begins her final stealthy approach. The chital stag is unaware of her presence. If she makes a sound his speed will ensure his escape. If he has time to turn at the last minute his needle-sharp antlers will create problems for her. It is a deadly game of chance; in Ranthambhore about one hunt in ten results in a kill.

later an adult chital stag moved down from the rise of a hill towards the stream bed, some 45 metres away from her. Again she froze and went into a crouch, carefully watching the unsuspecting deer. As he crossed her line she started her stalk, first moving on her belly a few metres at a time and then rising and moving with cautious stealth, effectively using the cover of shrubs and bushes. This movement of a tiger is without sound. The soft pads are placed on the ground slowly and with infinite care, each step taken with controlled precision as the muscles ripple. Head bent low, Nick Ear covered some 30 metres in 15 minutes. The chital stag was grazing at the edge of the stream bed. The distance between them closed until only seven or eight metres remained. The chital swung his head around, suspiciously sniffing the air, but could not spot the stalking tigress. He then climbed up an incline, and just then Nick Ear charged in pursuit. After a quick look behind him, the stag was off in a flash, again without an alarm call.

A frustrated Nick Ear climbed up the hill and across a large expanse of open grassland. It was nearly 6.00 p.m. and the sun was sinking below the horizon. She strode briskly and purposefully, but on approaching a deserted ruin she suddenly froze and dropped into a crouch. Some eight metres in front of her, around the ruin, grazed a herd of chital. She was lucky that she hadn't been spotted during her walk. She sat watching the herd for about three minutes then, moving on her belly, she crept forward. The herd was now only five metres away and I saw a quivering of her muscles as she bunched them. A few flicks of her tail, and then from this crouched position she took off in enormous bounds. For a second she appeared to fly. The chital, aware of serious danger, scattered; but one doe, in the confusion, rushed past the charging tigress who pounced on her – bringing her down and quickly shifting her grip to the nape of the neck. There was a choking squeak from the chital as the canines sank in. Nick Ear kept her grip for nearly three minutes and then, grabbing the chital by its neck, walked off with it, the chital's hind legs trailing on the ground.

Malik Talao is an interesting hunting ground. The lake and most of the meadows are bordered by a range of hills, and a maze of intersecting stream beds lead into the area. The lake itself is surrounded on all sides by tall grass, and I have often spent the whole day watching a tiger sitting patiently in the grass, waiting for an opportune moment to strike.

One day in November 1983 we received information that five tigers had slipped into the area along one of the stream beds. We rushed off, circling the

A tigress feeds on a chital doe, her claws extended to give added purchase as she tears at the carcass. A large male like Kublai could consume an adult chital in one night, but a tigress would probably eat the same amount more slowly, over two or three days. A large tiger can eat 30kg of meat in one sitting, and can then go without food for several days.

meadow. A few chital were grazing in the centre but of the tigers there was no sign. Our excitement was at a high pitch. Perhaps this could be the adult group we knew had been roaming the area for a few months. Switching off the engine we suddenly heard three frantic chital calls and then a choked squeak. Fateh, convinced that it was the death cry of a chital, moved to the spot. Just ahead of him, a tiger sat on its haunches, panting heavily.

We moved on, and as we crossed a patch of grass we encountered two more tigers. One was sitting with its paws hugging the carcass of a chital doe while the other watched alertly, moving a few steps forward. The first tiger emitted a low growl and then with a loud 'woof' charged at the second tiger. Both tigers rose briefly on their hind feet 'mock boxing' each other, but soon the second one rolled over on its back as if in submission. The first returned to the chital kill, followed closely by the second.

Fateh noticed that both were adult females. Woofing, coughing and growling, the two tigresses started pulling at the carcass from both ends in a regular tug-of-war, but the first tigress, pulling at the neck, seemed to be gaining ground. They moved some three or four metres in this strange manner until the first, and obviously more dominant of the two, let go of the carcass and leapt at the second tigress. The latter immediately released her grip and the dominant female again sat over the carcass as if hugging it. Low but ferocious growling emerged from her throat. Paws extending over the chital kill, she was vigorously asserting her rights over her prey.

The second tigress was now crawling towards the kill, burying her head alongside the paws of the first until her head was close to the carcass and near the neck of the first tigress. The first tigress now snarled viciously at the other, but it had no effect. Amazingly, they sat like this, without eating, for 30 minutes. The growling, coughing and snarling rose to a crescendo. I had never heard such a variety of tiger sounds before. It was aggression through sound, for at no time did the two animals attempt to actually injure each other.

Soon after this, the first tigress relinquished her hold and sat at the rump to start feeding. The second immediately went to the neck and did the same. The dominant one plucked out the tail of the carcass and then spat it out. It was the first time I had seen this happen though I have several times found a broken tail not far from a carcass. Tigers in Ranthambhore tend to pluck and spit out the tail before commencing to eat from the rump. In the event, the two tigresses ate ferociously from either side of the carcass, the dominant animal keeping up a continuous pitch of low growling. It was an unusual sight as rarely have I found two adults eating together. If sharing a kill, each one will normally await its turn so as to eat alone.

As they ate, their aggression manifested itself in great pulls from side to side and in 45 minutes the carcass appeared split at the centre, held together only by the skin. Eventually it broke in two, the rump being left with the dominant tigress and the neck, forelegs and chest with the second. They both crunched on for another 30 minutes while intestines, rumen and skin were all rapidly consumed. In the distance a mongoose nervously watched the activity.

At 5.15 p.m. this frantic eating was rudely interrupted by yet another tigress, who rose from her shady spot and charged the tigresses on the kill. To my surprise they quickly dispersed, leaving the entire remains to the third one, who immediately started feeding. I was sure she was the one we had seen panting earlier and thought it likely that she had killed the chital in the first place. However, she had permitted the other two females to eat before taking over.

Next morning we arrived to find just bits of bone. Even the skin around the skull had been chewed off and the only bones that remained were the hard ones. The carcass had been devastated. Even the few vultures circling around would find it difficult to collect any scraps. It was a remarkable situation. Interaction between tigers over a natural kill is a rare sight to observe and document. It has happened only a few times in our lives. C. McDougal, in his book *Face of the Tiger* (1977), states that on the 59 occasions on which he observed tigers feeding on bait, he never once

ABOVE Ears pressed back, coughing and snarling viciously, two tigresses struggle to establish a dominant position – and the right to eat first from the carcass of a chital doe. The two females were members of a larger group of five which we observed in November 1983.

encountered two adults feeding at the same time.

From my limited observation of tigers stalking, hunting and killing chital and sambar I find that the tiger takes more chances and risks with the chital. It charges greater distances and seems more confident about strategy, perhaps because of the size of the animal. Hunting the sambar tends to be a longer game of patience, and of varying tactics, and the tiger seems to want to get in much closer for the attempted kill. Nevertheless, the tiger kills more sambar than chital in Ranthambhore, even though the populations of the two species are much the same. This is probably due in part to the fact that the tiger and sambar are both diurnal in habit, and in part to the sambar's love of the water, which leads it into very vulnerable situations.

But the tiger is not the only predator that stalks the chital. The leopard also plays a key role in this, and in February 1979 I had probably my most memorable encounter with this animal. It was about 4.40 p.m. and the sun had lost its warmth. We had stopped the jeep on the brow of a hill overlooking the Semli valley. Soon we heard six or seven chital alarm calls, and sped towards their possible source. We found a few chital grazing but could see no sign of a predator. The chital had stopped calling, but suddenly Fateh spotted a leopard's head in a patch of grass. The small, elegant head merged in perfect harmony with the grass, providing almost perfect camouflage as it pivoted around, carefully watching the chital.

In the distance some sambar and a blue bull grazed. Suddenly the leopard darted towards an unsuspecting sambar fawn. But in vain. To our immense delight we discovered that the hunter was a leopardess, and she now emerged again from cover accompanied by her two cubs. They were half her size; one slightly bigger than the other. It was the first time ever that I had seen a leopardess with cubs, and I soon became so engrossed in their antics that I did not realize the leopardess was no longer in sight. The two youngsters dashed up a tree, leaping across from branch to branch. Then they scampered back down the trunk, and with a quick snarl at us moved off into a dry stream bed. As we turned the jeep around we saw a large male

ABOVE The usual 'one-at-a-time' feeding rule is broken occasionally, and here the same two tigresses struggle for possession of the carcass. Some minutes later a third tigress leapt out of cover and annexed the kill. At no time did the tigers actually fight; their aggression was expressed entirely in threats and vocalizations.

hyena loping across the track. Another rare sight, as the hyena in India is solitary and hardly ever seen.

Delighted at our luck, we had just decided to return to base when we found the leopardess only a few metres away – sitting with an adult chital stag she had just killed. I could not believe it. There we were, following the antics of the cubs in the tree while the mother, right behind us, had made her kill. I was sure the noise of the jeep must have helped her to stalk. Sad though we were to have missed the kill it still was a rare sight. She had just slit a layer of skin over the stomach – the characteristic method by which leopards start eating a kill.

The leopardess soon rose and moved off, while we prayed that she would return with her cubs for the feast. The forest was still and silent. The hyena was approaching. It must have smelt the kill. Alert and watchful he came up to the carcass and sniffed it, and then moved off some 30 metres or so. Suddenly, as if from nowhere, the leopardess was around him, hissing with rage as the animals circled each other. The stillness of the forest was shattered, and the valley of Semli echoed with the blood-curdling shrieks and moans of the hyena interspersed with the sharp coughs of the leopardess as they confronted each other. But to our amazement the leopardess soon gave way and climbed into a tree. I was stunned. I could not believe that a solitary hyena could get the better of a leopard. But so it was. The confrontation lasted late into the evening, but at no time did the leopardess launch a direct attack, or drive the hyena from her kill.

Eventually we decided to leave, having enjoyed five rare hours watching the hyena's prowess over the leopard. But I wondered why the leopardess hadn't tried to kill the hyena. Perhaps having her cubs around her kept her in a more submissive role. Whatever the reason for it, such an interaction in the wilds today is extremely rare, and I have found very few records of such happenings in the past. One of them is documented by Brander, who states that, 'Another animal which comes into the leopard's life is the hyena. He will often annex the leopard's kill and I have known them not only prevent

RIGHT The unlikely victor. After a short but violent confrontation this male hyena annexed the carcass of a chital stag by driving away the leopardess who had made the kill. The hyena ripped open the carcass and gorged himself for 40 minutes, blood dripping from his jaws. At one stage he tried to drag the carcass away but it was too heavy for him.

ABOVE As soon as the hyena moved away, the distraught leopardess rushed back to her kill and started to eat. But within minutes the hyena returned. Once more the forest exploded with blood-curdling snarls and shrieks as the two battled over the carcass. And once again it was the leopardess who was forced to retreat. It is the only direct leopard-hyena interaction I have ever seen — and the outcome was quite unexpected. There have been very few accounts of such happenings in the past.

LEFT Crocodiles are quick to scavenge the carcasses of any animals that die of natural causes around the shores of the lakes. Here, one of the large (three metre) dominant crocodiles chases a smaller one from the carcass of a chital stag.

BELOW The bloated carcass is dragged into the water where the dominant crocodile starts to wrench it apart. The legs are usually attacked first and are torn off with a violent twisting motion powered by the crocodile's massive tail.

the leopard coming up, but even to attack him on the kill and drive him off. The leopard seems to recognize his master, and this is the more curious as they will readily kill a dog as big as a hyena.'

Some chital fawns fall prey to the crocodile, and twice has this been observed on the Ranthambhore lakes. But more often the crocodiles scavenge on the carcasses of animals that have died naturally. In early April 1985 a chital stag was found dead on the shore of Rajbagh. A small crocodile approached the carcass from the water at noon but could not move it and slithered away. A slightly bigger one came an hour later and attempted to twist the stomach of the chital in an effort to open the carcass. It, too, was unsuccessful, but its activity caused the arrival of several larger crocodiles, the largest of which quickly moved onto the shore and, taking a firm grip on the chital's rump, dragged it back into the water.

Five or six crocodiles swarmed around the dominant one in the water. The carcass was floating and the dominant crocodile repeatedly chased the others away in an effort to protect his trophy. This activity continued for nearly an hour. The dominant crocodile then commenced chewing on one of the hind legs of the chital. This seemed to signal an invitation to the other crocodiles and amidst much splashing they all joined in the feast. The carcass drifted farther out into the lake and soon little could be seen.

THE WILD BOAR

One hot summer afternoon, while walking through the deserted ruins of the lake palace, I heard a noisy rustling of grass and a group of six wild boars rushed past me grunting furiously. I was rooted to the spot with surprise, frozen for the moment. My thoughts drifted to this much maligned and much shot-at species of our wilds.

The Indian wild boar is allied to the European wild boar but is distinctive because of its sparser coat and the fuller crest or mane of black bristles extending from the nape of its neck, down the back. It is basically black in colour with grey, rusty brown and some white hairs. The young are browner with light or black stripes. A well-grown mature male can stand 90 centimetres high at the shoulder and its weight can exceed 225 kilogrammes. The tusks can be well developed in the males, with both the upper and lower tusks curving outwards, projecting from the mouth. The record measurement for a pair of lower tusks is nearly 32 centimetres along the outside curve, and large tusks were much-prized hunting trophies in the days of *shikar*. However, I have never seen such large tusks in the dry deciduous forests of Ranthambhore and there is probably a tremendous variation in size between one forest and another.

Boars are very widely distributed. They are found over virtually the entire sub-continent, in Burma, Thailand and parts of the Malay Peninsula, and are also quite common in Sri Lanka. Though only a single species is found in India today, there were six or seven species in the Eocene Period — roughly 70 million years to 40 million years ago — one of them in the shape of a huge monster.

Boars generally prefer to inhabit grass and shrub country, though sometimes they are also found in quite dense forests. In Ranthambhore their population fluctuates markedly as the animals move over considerable distances into and out of the Park. The average population of the Park and surrounding area is probably at least 2,000, and our observations indicate that this is the third most commonly taken tiger prey species in the Ranthambhore forest.

The open grasslands and shrub country of Ranthambhore is ideal boar habitat and I have often seen them around the edges of the lakes, feeding, digging and wallowing in the mud. They tend to be nervous and shy and take off at speed when approached. They are omnivorous by habit, living on crops, roots, insects, snakes, offal and carrion, with a tendency to feed in the early morning and late evening. They also play an important role in the forest as scavengers. I have seen them feeding on the carcasses of spotted deer and sambar, both of which had died of natural causes, and once saw a large

In the heat of summer, 1985, a large sambar stag collapsed and died in a sun-baked clearing in the Ranthambhore forest. The dead stag provided a focal point for four days of feeding activity in which we were able to study at close range the natural hierarchy and interactions of Ranthambhore's scavengers.

ABOVE Day 1: We arrived early in the morning to find the area around the carcass criss-crossed by crocodile tracks. The reptiles had managed only to tear a chunk of flesh from the sambar's neck before retreating into a nearby pool. It was a lucky break for the vultures; white-backed, Egyptian, king, griffon and long-billed vultures all congregated to feed, tearing at the carcass through the opening made by the crocodiles and all the time flapping, kicking and fighting amongst themselves.

LEFT Day 2: A couple of jackals arrived at the scene, approaching cautiously and then charging the vultures and chasing them off. They fed on and off throughout the day, but as evening fell they too were forced to retreat as the carcass was annexed by a group of four wild boars.

BOTTOM LEFT Day 3: The boars were firmly established as the dominant scavengers: vultures and jackals kept well away and even the ever-present tree-pies and crows found it difficult to snatch any scraps.

Day 4: Evidence left in the dusty soil indicated the arrival during the night of a tigress. She had picked up the remains of the carcass and dragged them 30m away into some bushes where she had chewed on the limbs and licked the bones clean. In just four days the stag had been reduced to scraps of bone.

tusker feeding on the leftovers of a tiger kill. When scavenging in a group, the dominant male is extremely aggressive towards the others and will invariably take the largest share.

The boars' sense of smell is acute but their eyesight and hearing are only moderate. They breed in all seasons and are known to collect in large assemblies of up to 200 animals, especially while pairing. In Ranthambhore I have seen gatherings of nearly fifty during courtship and have also observed two adult boars charging and fighting each other over the females and grunting ferociously. They sometimes rear up on their hind legs to fight and I have seen females do this also. The victor of such a clash between males spends much of his time sniffing and pushing the female with his snout, and just once have I seen a pair copulating. The loser, meanwhile, remains on the fringes of the group waiting for another opportunity.

During this period there is incessant activity amongst the males to establish their hierarchy. A dominant male will lead the group while the females are receptive, but once the breeding period is over the adult males tend to lead solitary lives, coming together again in large groups only when the sows are on heat. Several times I have encountered solitary males roaming the forest.

The gestation period of a boar is believed to be four months, and four to eight young can be born at a time. In Ranthambhore, a majority of the young are born between July and September and I have frequently seen the tiny, striped, new-born young. The sow shelters her litter in a heaped-up mound of grass or branches, a structure which she builds before giving birth. She keeps a close watch on her offspring for many months and is a most aggressively protective mother, diligently keeping her young away from the teeth and claws of predators as the defenceless little piglets make easy and succulent prey.

Over the last couple of centuries, sportsmen and naturalists have stressed that this heavy, squat, clumsy animal is a great delicacy for the tiger. I cannot confirm or deny this from my own field experience, but I do know that tigers attack and kill wild boars quite frequently and that very little is left to waste. Predation on the wild boar seems to have increased steeply in the last five years, especially since the tiger began its daylight activities. All around the lakes are patches of high grass and scrub where the wild boar is often to be seen. Tigers, too, frequent the long grass, sitting concealed, waiting to pounce. Being squat and with only moderate hearing and eyesight, the boars make an easy target. A sounder of boars reacts in total

RIGHT Laxmi studies three young boars from the far side of a clearing. It is a moment loaded with tension, but she is in no hurry. She knows that their vision is poor and their speed no match for hers so she is prepared to start her charge from quite some distance away. The victim, if caught, will usually be knocked down by a blow from her paw before being seized by the neck.

confusion to a tiger's charge and this gives an additional advantage to the tiger. But, as we have seen, the tiger is by no means always successful.

One morning in late November 1982 I am driving around Rajbagh and on switching off the engine discover that both langurs and spotted deer are calling continuously. Moving ahead, I find a tigress striding along the road. It is Nick Ear. She stops, rolls on her back, gets up and walks on for about 30 metres, spray-marking four trees. Six peacocks watch her as she turns off the road and moves into tall grass. We circle the grass and find her about to exit from the far side. A slight movement in the grass distracts her. She turns, now totally alert, and darts back into the grass. A female wild boar is standing outside the patch of grass. The tigress watches her for a second and then charges in. I hear a squeak and two striped piglets rush out of the grass with Nick Ear in full pursuit. She flashes past the sow, only a couple of metres away, and focusses on one of the piglets. In seconds her forepaws come pounding down on the tiny animal.

Instantly, she grips the piglet by the nape of the neck and carries it off into the grass. Several quail rush out in panic. The sow watches. Nick Ear eats a bit but then decides to carry her prey deeper into the grass. The sow comes in closer, looking anxiously into the thicket. It is 8.30 a.m. I find it quite incredible that the tigress should choose the tiny piglet instead of the mother. Perhaps it is tastier. For the next three hours I continue to watch the grass. A few chital are grazing in the distance. A lone crow caws from the branch of a tree. From behind us the sow emerges again moving towards the grass. Spotting us she stops and retreats.

At 1.20 p.m. I see the sow moving into the grass again. She has gone barely ten metres when there is a loud thrashing around and I see the tiger's head appear as she bounds in pursuit. But with much grunting the boar scuttles away to safety. It is always amazing to watch the plight of a mother when her piglet has been killed. She conducts a suicidal search for it, even

ABOVE A tiger with a large male wild boar he has just over-powered. The boar's tusks are a formidable weapon and the tiger must have struck swiftly and accurately to stun or kill the boar without suffering any injury in the confrontation.

through tall grass which she must know conceals a tiger. This motherly instinct is also found among the sambar and chital who react in much the same way when their fawns are killed.

While driving to Malik Talao one morning in December 1984, Fateh spotted a king vulture sitting in a tree. It was in an open grassy meadow and after much investigation we found Laxmi sitting in the grass with a young boar, the rump of which she had already eaten. It was 8.00 a.m. At 2.00 p.m. she rose and moved a few steps to the carcass, sniffed it and dragged it a few metres. She then sat and ate for about 15 minutes, by which time the carcass was half eaten. She then moved off and slept under the shade of a tree. At 5.00 p.m. some chital approached the area. Laxmi crouched, and moved a few paces on her belly. The chital came within ten metres of her, but she didn't charge.

It was now dark and we left. On returning the next morning we found a pair of king vultures on the side of the carcass – a sure sign of an absent tigress. The wild boar had not been touched since the previous day. Half of it was completely intact. We spent much time looking around the meadow for the tigress, but in vain. I was really puzzled. After all these years I was seeing the desertion of a kill by a tiger. But I couldn't fathom the reason. Fateh got off the jeep and examined the kill. The marks of Laxmi's canines were on the nape of the neck. There was a big gash around the shoulder as if the tigress had smacked it sharply with her paw before actually killing it. The choicest bits were eaten. But a lot of meat remained. Mystified by for this desertion we returned to base, watching the vultures descend.

The large male boar with its heavy body and protective tusks has always been regarded as difficult prey for tiger and leopard alike. But from my field observations I have never encountered a situation where the tiger avoided a confrontation with a boar. In fact our records document two tiger kills of male boars. I have never found a leopard with a boar kill and have no observations of this predator and the boar, but old etchings do show combat between the two. Very rarely did a leopard win a fight with a large boar.

Old accounts of interactions between adult boars and tigers leave no doubt at all that the boar is a courageous and daunting adversary, and that such confrontations were invariably bloody and uncompromising affairs. In most encounters the boar faced the tiger with hair and bristles erect, wheeling around with its head lowered. The tiger, ears back and crouched low, would circle the boar then suddenly spring forward, attempting to strike a crippling blow with its paw. But the boar, even though squat and heavy, is very agile. In fact, any weakness on the part of the tiger is exploited by the boar who charges instantly with all its weight, attempting to drive its tusks into the tiger's side or belly. Even when dripping with blood and with bits of skin hanging from gaping wounds, the boar will not give up. The tiger attempts to tear out chunks of flesh, but if he is at all inexperienced the boar is likely to wound or even disembowel him with its flashing tusks. Tiger and boar, bleeding, wounded and exhausted, face each other. The tiger is the first to limp off into thicker forest, followed by the boar. Both will later die of their wounds.

Many writers, including Caldwell (1925) and Hanley (1961), have recorded that when a group of wild boars is threatened by the presence of a tiger or leopard, the males range themselves like a protective wall and the predator, confronted by such a formidable barrier, generally retreats. On one occasion Hanley observed a tiger preparing to spring on a group of wild boars when suddenly a spotted deer let out its alarm call and the wild boars spotted the tiger. The boars instantly formed a protective screen while the young ones scattered for shelter. The tiger rose slowly, looked up in disgust and sauntered off.

The remarkable courage of the wild boar is just as likely to be displayed in the face of human persecution as it is towards the boar's natural enemies in the forest. Pig-sticking was an odious sport, popular in the days of British rule, in which boars were pursued on horseback until finally speared to death. But many of those who indulged in the sport found to their cost just how dangerous an injured boar could be.

—————————— THE NILGAI OR BLUE BULL ——————————

The nilgai, or blue bull, is the largest antelope native to Asia, and fossil remains testify to the fact that it was a very early inhabitant of the Indian sub-continent. Today it is found in most parts of India except for Bengal, Assam and the Malabar Coast. It flourishes in sparsely vegetated hill country and in flat undulating grassland, making the terrain of Ranthambhore an ideal refuge.

The nilgai is a large ungainly creature, rather horse-like in appearance with high withers and a low rump. Yet despite its size and appearance the animal can move very fast — especially once it has accelerated to a full gallop. An adult male can weigh well over 270 kilogrammes, and while cows and young males are tawny in colour, the adult male has a coarse iron-grey coat with two white spots on either side of the cheek and a white ring below each fetlock. Other touches of white are found on the lips, the chin, the inside of the ears and on the underside of the tail. The dark mane is common to both sexes but the male also has a tuft of steel-black hair on the throat. Bulls have stout conical horns which are distinctly keeled, triangular at the base and circular towards the tip. I have only once found a female with horns.

Today, nilgais are not found in very large numbers within the forests of Ranthambhore, and their population of about 1,800 is concentrated mainly in the open and grassy areas. They do not mind the hot sun, and feed most of the day on the fruits and leaves of various trees. Usually, nilgai move in groups of ten to fifteen but sometimes the members can swell to about twenty. Young males can exist within these groups but upon nearing maturity they tend to separate, sometimes to lead solitary lives and sometimes accompanied by one or two other males. Adult and mature males attempt to join and take over a group as soon as the females are in oestrus.

The height of the nilgai's rutting period in Ranthambhore is November. This is when mature males will clash over females but these conflicts are more time-consuming than vicious. Two adult bulls will circle each other with tails raised, vocalizing with grunts. This circling movement can go on for over an hour before the less dominant of the males decides to retreat from the fray. The dominant male then chases his defeated opponent a long way from the area, and rapidly returns to his harem. I have seen him chasing a beaten male for 500 metres, but only once have I observed actual combat between males. The process is unusual. Two adult bulls will kneel on their forelegs, sparring with each other and exerting great pressure with their horns. Often they will entwine their necks in an effort to push each other away. However, competing adult males often avoid direct confrontation by keeping their distance. I once saw a young male submitting several times before an adult thus preventing the possibility of conflict. The young male would lower his head, attempting to tuck it in the hind area of the adult and the two males would then lick each other and part. This process may continue for up to 30 minutes.

Nilgai have an interesting habit of regularly using the same spot to deposit their droppings. They select clear, open areas for this activity. According to Brander, such spots are used as rendezvous points at which the herd can reassemble if it becomes scattered during the night. He goes on to say that nilgais indulge in peculiar behaviour when assembling in such places. Considerable jealousy is displayed over these spots, with one animal rushing in and driving off another while it relieves itself.

Courting is again done with much licking and sniffing before copulation. Fateh once spotted a female kneeling on her forelegs before the male and then prancing around him to arouse his feelings. The male pursued the female, with much effort at copulation and licking. He was disturbed in his courtship by a competing male but successfully chased the intruder away. Copulation is often brief and can take place at regular intervals. The gestation period of the nilgai is about eight or nine months and mothers take great care of their young, suckling them with great regularity. One or two young are born at the same time.

The animal's Indian name means 'blue cow', and as the antelope is regarded as sacred it has virtually nothing to offer the *shikari*. In fact it is very rarely shot. The nilgai's senses are moderately developed compared with those of the deer; they have fair powers of sight and smell but not such good hearing. If attacked by dogs they protect themselves by rearing up on their hind feet and striking blows with their forefeet. The danger of predation to the adult nilgai seems to come only from the tiger, and it is the fourth most common species eaten by the tiger in Ranthambhore. When suspicious and conscious of danger, the nilgai emits a low grunting alarm call which alerts the group. This call is normally a good indication of the presence of a tiger as nilgais seldom call without good reason. Being large animals they are no easy prey for the tiger and our observations of interaction between tiger and nilgai are limited.

On a warm April evening in 1979, when the sun had just set over the hills, we were driving back to base when Fateh whispered, 'tiger'. Stopping the jeep, he pointed to the silhouette of a tiger as it rushed down a low cliff beside the road. The forest was without alarm. The tiger stopped some ten metres away from the jeep and took shelter in a large bush, all crouched up. I was surprised for a moment, not realizing what this male tiger was up to, when it suddenly dawned on me that he must have spotted something from the cliff and positioned himself strategically.

We crossed our fingers in expectation. There was a rustling in the grass; the sound of animals moving. The tiger froze. Around the corner of the cliff came a female nilgai with two young ones. The young ones led, followed by the female, without an inkling of the tiger's presence. They passed close to the bush, and when the mother was just a few metres away, the tiger shifted, crouched and leapt out at her in one bound. In one smooth flowing motion his paws struck the back of the animal and his canines made for the nape. This initial leap carried enough momentum to bring down the nilgai and the tiger quickly shifted his grip from the nape of the neck to the throat. Life ebbed out of the animal in less than a minute but the tiger kept its grip for five minutes. He then let go and proceeded to drag his victim by the neck some six or seven metres to a patch of long grass. In a few minutes he began eating from the rump, and I could hear his canines tearing at the flesh. After eating for about 20 minutes he proceeded carefully to lick the rear of the animal. I

ABOVE A young male nilgai bows his head in submission before an older, more dominant male. Only when he is older, bigger and more powerful will he stand any chance of taking over a harem.

RIGHT A young female nilgai peers out through long grass, her brown and white markings blending into the light and shade patterns of the forest edge.

ABOVE A male nilgai attempts to mount a female who, in the manner characteristic of her species, appears totally unconcerned about what is going on.

LEFT The female nilgai is a caring and protective mother – always alert to the threat of attack by jackals and other predators. Like the female sambar and chital she suckles her calf frequently.

have found that when eating, tigers do much licking with their coarse tongues, especially around the head of the animal when that is all that is left.

The most exciting encounter I ever witnessed involving tiger and nilgai took place on a chilly November morning in 1982. We are driving around the third lake when in the distance we see a frantic tracker on a bicycle, gesticulating wildly as he approaches us. He shouts, 'There is a tree full of crows and I have just seen a tiger eating on a blue bull by Rajbagh.' We rush off and sure enough come to a tree with nearly fifty crows on it. Below it sits Padmini with three 14-month-old cubs around her. Nearby lies the carcass of a huge adult male bull which must weigh at least 250 kilogrammes, possibly more. The carcass is far too heavy for her to move and Padmini is nibbling at the rump, a small portion of which has been eaten. The two cubs sitting behind her get up in an attempt to approach the kill, but as they come close she rises, coughs sharply and slaps one of them across the face. The cub submits, rolling over on its back, and settles down near her restlessly while the other cub starts to eat from the rump. Padmini seems to be saying, quite clearly, 'One at a time.'

At 7.30 a.m. Padmini gets up, grabs the nilgai by the neck and tries to drag it away, but its foot gets stuck in a forked tree root. She settles down to eat some more, and half an hour later tries again – this time dragging the carcass about eight metres. Now she permits the second cub to eat. The third lies some 30 metres away in the distance. Crows chatter incessantly and a group of vultures circle while others sit on a nearby tree. The crows fly in and around in an attempt to pick up scraps of meat but twice Padmini charges them. A single vulture flops down but in a flash he too is charged and takes flight.

Soon after this, Padmini drags the carcass about ten metres farther up the rise of a hill. We follow quickly as the terrain is easy here and accessible to a jeep. The great advantage of dhok forest is its excellent visibility, and scanning the area we now see Laxmi, Padmini's female cub from her litter of 1976. We now have five tigers spread out at different distances around the carcass, Padmini and Laxmi closest to it. There is much getting up and sitting down and Laxmi twice marks the trunk of a tree. Now Padmini gets up, sniffs a tree, spray-marks it and walks towards her nearest cub, nuzzling it briefly. She then turns around and walks past Laxmi, snarling at her before grabbing the neck of the nilgai and pulling it farther up the hill. Two of her cubs are sleeping in the distance, but soon all three rise and circle out of sight. Padmini and Laxmi are lying side by side near the carcass.

A few minutes later Padmini gets up and walks down the slope of the hill towards the lake. Laxmi moves towards the carcass and starts to feed. It is 11.00 a.m. We follow Padmini as she moves towards the edge of the second lake and flops into a patch of water. She drinks a little, rolls around and gives herself a good soaking. After 20 minutes she rises and moves into the long grass. Sounds of snarling and growling are heard and the faint outline of two tigers can be seen moving in it. Padmini soon emerges from the grass and sits by the roadside.

We leave her there and go back to the nilgai. Laxmi is eating but surprisingly there is now another adult tigress sitting nearby. It is Nick Ear, a female from Padmini's second litter. At noon Padmini appears from the rear, marks a tree and moves towards the kill. She and Laxmi cough at each other. Padmini sits, and snarls at Laxmi who moves off towards Nick Ear and settles down on her side to sleep. Padmini also dozes off but with a watchful eye on the crows perched on the branches. At 12.30 p.m. the dominant cub returns from the lakeside and sits at the kill, nibbling at the fast-diminishing rump while Padmini watches alertly.

At 1.00 p.m. the cub moves off and rolls on his back before flopping on his side to sleep. Padmini gets up and chews on the carcass for some 15 minutes, then she too moves off again towards the lake. Laxmi rises and settles near the carcass. At 2.00 p.m. Padmini returns to her original position and a grimacing Laxmi moves back. From our rear two more of the cubs emerge. There are now six tigers in front of us. The sight is unbelievable.

RIGHT Padmini displays the incredible power of a mature tiger as she drags the carcass of a 250kg male nilgai up a wooded slope. It was around this kill, in November 1982, that we witnessed the remarkable sight of nine tigers feeding under the control of a single tigress – Padmini herself.

BELOW One of Padmini's sub-adult cubs stands by the carcass while Padmini sleeps nearby. A crow has just landed on the carcass – but will be chased off immediately. Jungle crows are a great help to us in the forest. Many times they have led us to fresh kills.

RIGHT Find the tiger! This remarkable photograph, taken by Fateh, shows the absolute perfection of the tiger's camouflage. To the left, Laxmi feeds on the remains of the nilgai; Padmini lies asleep in the foreground; two of Padmini's sub-adult cubs are sprawled in the grass ahead, and another watches cautiously from the background.

But more is to come. About 45 metres away, amidst growling and snarling, yet another female, Nasty, appears – growling continuously as she approaches the carcass. The seventh tiger; but this time one without any kin-link to Padmini. Time seems to stand still, but then at 3.00 p.m. we spot a large male walking along the edge of the hill. He sits down some distance away, and after carefully studying him with our binoculars we discover that it is Akbar, the dominant male of Padmini's first litter. And behind him, with thudding hearts, we see yet another tiger, but at this range we cannot identify it.

Fateh and I look at each other in near hysteria. Nine tigers surround us at varying distances from the nilgai. Hardly daring to breathe, our eyes switch from tiger to tiger. No eating is taking place. Four are sleeping, two are grooming, and two are watching the kill. One is on its back, paws in the air. Padmini seems to be completely in command of the group and is obviously the one who killed the nilgai. Soon after 3.30 p.m. Nick Ear moves towards the kill and eats for some 25 minutes. She then moves off and Padmini's dominant cub arrives to feast. Laxmi also decides to eat but a sharp snarl from Padmini sends her off. After the cub has eaten for 15 minutes he moves off, and Laxmi comes in to eat.

So far we have seen five different tigers eating, but only one at a time and all strictly controlled by Padmini. There seem to be one male and two females in her third litter. Laxmi now moves off towards a dry stream bed from where chital alarm calls are sounding. Perhaps her own cubs are hidden there as we have seen no sign of them. She vocalizes six times before moving out of sight. The time is 4.30 p.m. and the shades of evening are taking over. At 5.20 p.m. we leave the hill after some ten uninterrupted hours of quite extraordinary observation. The next morning, on returning at 7.00 a.m., I find five tigers; Laxmi, Padmini and her three cubs, sitting around the kill with just the head and rib cage of the nilgai left. After chewing for 40 minutes they disappear over a rise and into a *nallah*.

Now only the crows are left, picking at bits of bone. We leave. It has been an incredible 24 hours. I have never come across a description of a scene like the one we have just witnessed – where nine tigers have fed on the same carcass, totally controlled by a dominant female. It would appear that Padmini had made the kill but as several other tigers were also present in the area she took a decision to share the carcass. As it happened, all except two of the tigers were sons and daughters from her various litters. But she had total control and dominance over the situation. Not once did she permit two tigers to eat together, thereby preventing the conflict that could have arisen.

To find nine tigers around a kill is a rarity, and I think the fact that seven were related means that there is the possibility of strong kinship links among

ABOVE 5 March 1985: News of a tigress reaches us from Bakaula. She has been sighted with a kill which, to our delight, is a female nilgai – a prey species around which we have had few opportunities to see tigers feeding. On nearing the site we find the Bakaula tigress quenching her thirst at a small stream, lapping at the water for over five minutes.

RIGHT Tigers visit the water quite frequently while feeding on a kill, both to drink and to soak themselves. But despite their love of the water they very rarely get the face wet. The usual method of entry is to reverse into the water very slowly and carefully, always remaining facing the bank.

RIGHT Tigers will tolerate no interference at all with their kills. A couple of crows and some tree-pies have landed behind the bushes where the Bakaula tigress has hidden her nilgai. In a flash she charges from the water, sending the birds into the air in panic.

RIGHT Having chased off the birds, the tigress wheels round to check for any other intrusion – her fury still clear from the vicious snarl contorting her face. With a huge effort she then dragged the heavy carcass up a hill into dense cover where she remained for the next four days – feeding, and leaving the kill only to come down to the stream to drink.

tigers and that these may be sustained over long periods of time. I think tigers easily recognize another individual, be it brother, sister or mother. A great deal more observation is needed for conclusive evidence on kinship links and their role. But this example shows that tigers can congregate without conflict around a natural kill – and with a female in full control of the feeding process.

THE LANGUR

The langur is the only primate that exists within the forest of Ranthambhore. It is believed to have evolved some ten to twelve million years ago. In India there are four subspecies, the one found in Ranthambhore being the Hanuman or common langur, which abounds in large numbers especially around temples and villages. In Ranthambhore, most of the troops are quite shy, being forest dwellers. Their total population numbers about 2,000.

The range of this primate extends over most of India from the Himalayas to Cape Comorin except for the western deserts and Sri Lanka. In the Himalayas, langurs inhabit forests up to altitudes of nearly 3,700 metres. They are extremely adaptable, and are even able to live in very dry areas where in summer there is little water beyond that which exists in the leaves and bark on which the animals feed. However, in more productive habitats the langurs feed on a wide variety of buds, fruits, flowers, shoots and leaves, and occasionally also insects.

When seated, the langur is about 60 centimetres high, and adults weigh up to 16 kilogrammes. They are long-limbed, with long tails and black faces, and are venerated in India by the Hindus. Consequently the langurs are seldom molested. They have excellent eyesight and are able to spot predators very easily from their perches high in the trees. On seeing a predator they immediately emit a sharp, raucous, resounding bark which is a useful guide to observers looking for tigers or leopards. Langurs also react very promptly to the alarm calls of other animals, particularly those of the peacock and red-wattled lapwing which abound in the forest.

Socially, langurs are divided into two groups. In the first type, a troop consists of 15 to 25 members and includes an adult dominant male, seven or eight females and several immature animals. The dominant male leads the troop, which moves according to his signals over an area of two to ten square kilometres, containing several favourite perching trees. The second type of group comprises an all-male band of between six and fifteen langurs made up of several adult and immature animals. These male bands attempt to invade the normal troops in an effort to displace the dominant males. If successful, the dominant male of the male band takes control of the harem – a dangerous situation in which infanticide can take place. The reason for this is that if a dominant male is displaced, and in most cases he is either killed or severely injured, the new male will attempt to kill the infants of the troop in order to bring his harem rapidly back into breeding condition. I saw this once in December 1983 in Ranthambhore. While watching a tiger in the grass at Rajbagh I suddenly noticed a commotion at the far side of the lake. I saw a galloping male monkey carrying a limp infant in its mouth being chased by two females. He dropped his prey after a short chase and the females quickly picked it up and rushed into the cover of a tree. As far as I could see the infant showed no sign of life.

At the approach of an invading male band, the dominant male of a troop will vocalize by whooping and occasionally even cackle-barking. Sometimes there is much gnashing of teeth between opposing males, followed by a long chase as the male of the troop attempts to chase away the intruder. Langurs also whoop at times, jumping from tree to tree, when the noise of a jeep disturbs them. They are agile and very precise in their leaps and bounds, and it is fun to watch their acrobatic performance.

The langurs' mating season is between April and September and gestation lasts for six to seven months. Most of the young are born after December but there are exceptions to this and I have occasionally seen infants in September and October, and several times in March. The mother is caring and protective of her infants and she often carries them clinging to her belly fur. The newly born young are nurtured by several females of a troop in their first weeks. As they grow, infants develop their characteristic grey hair and are exceptionally playful – jumping, bounding and somersaulting all over the place. They tug at each others' tails and indulge in acrobatic mock fights.

The langur has two main predators in Ranthambhore, the tiger and the leopard, the latter being generally regarded as the major one. Direct observations of leopard predation are rare, but we have on many occasions witnessed the reactions of langurs when a leopard is close at hand. I once came upon a leopard walking along an animal path and passing beneath a tree full of langurs. Immediately they started their cackle-barking, jumping from branch to branch in great agitation until the leopard was out of sight. In fact I could still hear them barking even after the leopard had moved some half a kilometre away. Langurs have this tendency to continue calling even after a predator has moved away. On another occasion Fateh witnessed a 'near miss' on the edge of the Park near the town of Sawai Madhopur. While driving down to the forest late one evening he spotted a leopard rapidly ascending a tree full of langurs. The leopard clambered up the branches chasing the monkeys but amidst much cackle-barking and jumping around the monkeys managed to flee to an adjoining tree and the leopard gave up its pursuit and moved away.

A langur mother suckles her young infant. She is an exceptionally protective and caring mother, and within the troop other females too will share the responsibility of caring for the young.

A time for relaxation. In the relative safety of a huge old banyan tree a group of langurs while away the afternoon — some dozing, others grooming each other's fur in a ritual that cleans the fur of lice and other pests and also reinforces the bonds within the troop.

ABOVE Two young langurs chase each other in a high-speed game of 'catch'. The langur's long tail is a very effective balancing organ and plays an important role in the monkey's acrobatic activities both on the ground and high in the forest canopy.

Fateh has on three different occasions arrived to find a tiger departing from a langur kill. The langur is a small prey species which can be consumed quickly, and after a tiger has fed on it scarcely anything remains. Once he found Laxmi leaving a langur kill, carrying away the tail in her mouth! I have only once found the remnants of a kill and that was just minutes after two tigers had left it. All that remained was the skull, a few bones and one hand.

One day late in February, in 1983, I spent several hours with Nick Ear who was dozing in the shade of a large bush at the corner of Padam Talao. She was about 30 metres away from a pool of water. At 4.15 p.m. a troop of langurs emerged from behind me, walking along the grassy terrain towards the water-hole. Nick Ear watched alertly. Suddenly she crouched and moved forward a few paces on her belly. As the langurs crossed her path some twelve metres or so away she sprang from her crouch and charged. The six or eight langurs in front of her rushed towards a tree, rapidly ascending it. Nick Ear was only a metre or so behind the last monkey as it hurled itself desperately into the tree. He escaped by a hair's breadth, leaving Nick Ear furiously swiping at the swaying branch onto which he clung.

However, the most remarkable interaction between tiger and langur which I ever saw occurred one afternoon in January 1985 when we drove to Malik Talao. Some 35 to 40 sambar were standing half-immersed in the water, quietly grazing on the grasses and water weeds at the lake edge. Suddenly a single sambar alarm call startled the whole herd into panic. They rushed from the water in a flurry of spray leaving just three of their number behind. But the alarm call was not repeated.

We circled the lake to find Noon sitting on the shore farther along, but as we neared her she moved off into the tall grass surrounding the lake, startling a hare which leapt out and fled from her. I followed and with some difficulty spotted her in a thick clump of grass, fast asleep. Her camouflage was so good that at five metres the only thing to be seen was the white of her underbelly and one ear. We stayed with her until 3.10 p.m. and then moved away for an hour, returning to find her position unchanged.

Half an hour later I noticed a troop of langurs behind her, jumping about in the branches of a tree and feeding on ber fruit. Noon briefly raised her head to watch them but then went back to sleep. After a few minutes a large langur came out of the undergrowth as if to go towards the lake for water. It was walking through tall grass and I noticed how close it was getting to the tigress. Sure enough it would pass within five metres of her.

Noon suddenly came awake, disturbed by the rustling of the grass. Instantly, she spotted the langur and from a crouched position took one bound, followed by a flashing leap, and seemed to fall directly onto the defenceless monkey. For that split second the langur was stunned: paralysed by the sight of this leaping apparition. Noon seemed to pinion the monkey first with her forepaws and then took a grip on its rear flank with her canines. The monkey shrieked, struggling furiously against the tiger's grip. We watched in stunned silence, our view partly obstructed by the tall grass. Swiftly Noon shifted her grip. Her canines closed into the neck and in seconds the monkey was silenced. She now rose, holding the dead langur firmly by the neck, and stayed frozen like this for some three minutes before moving off into the long grass to feed.

I jumped on to the bonnet of the jeep to record this rare sight. The killing of a langur is probably the rarest predation of all, and to have witnessed it at first hand was incredibly good luck. Up in the trees langurs are safe from the tiger, but when they descend to the ground – and particularly when crossing open ground to drink at a water-hole – they are very vulnerable. In this instance the langur had been caught right in the open. As Noon fed, the rest of the langur troop climbed into a tree, gave a few sporadic alarm calls, and then sat in silence as if stunned by grief.

We soon left, only to find a large male langur striding down the road in the direction of the troop, which seemed to have lost its dominant male. It is uncanny how the dominant individual of a male band arrives within hours to take over a troop that has lost its leader!

BELOW A langur in mid-leap. The monkeys are remarkably acrobatic and agile, and fall prey to the tiger only when caught on the ground in the open, for example when approaching a water-hole to drink.

LEFT Noon strides off into long grass to feed – her canines still clenched in the killing grip several minutes after life has ebbed from the langur. This is a very rare photograph. Although langurs form a regular part of the tiger's diet in Ranthambhore it is very unusual to witness the kill, and because the body is small it is rare to find a tiger with a carcass: the 12-15kg monkey is usually consumed immediately.

LEFT Noon feeds on her langur kill, well concealed in the cover of tall grass. A scavenging tree-pie hovers above her in a state of agitation – pin-pointing exactly the tigress's position. These noisy and conspicuous birds are a great help to observers trying to locate tigers and leopards in the thick cover of grass, bush and forest.

I was sure that Noon would eat the twelve kilogrammes or so of meat very quickly, and move off during the night. However, I was very surprised to find her in exactly the same spot the next morning. She spent more than 24 hours in the same area, taking her time over eating the kill, resting in the grass and occasionally walking around or moving down to the lake for a drink. At one point we watched her pause at a sandy spot on the road and eat the soil for several minutes — an action we have seen a number of times before and which, presumably, aids the tiger's digestive system.

THE PEAFOWL

Peafowl inhabit the forest of Ranthambhore in their thousands, their resplendent plumage illuminating the whole forest. From April onwards the cock birds dance, courting the peahens throughout the summer months. Yet despite their great numbers and size, these beautiful birds are rarely seen in the act of mating. I have never seen it. Fateh, with all his years in the forest has seen it just once. At the culmination of the spectacular courtship dance the peacock mounts the hen, his feathers forming a huge fan which gently falls over her. At this time of year the peacocks also fight for supremacy. Two peacocks will face each other and then quite suddenly jump into the air, kicking their feet and wings outwards. They do this several times before the less dominant bird leaves the fray. This, too, is a rare sight and I have only seen it once. The eggs are laid during the rains and soon after, and peahens with their young are commonly seen in September and October.

Peafowl are well dispersed through the forest and can be found around bushy, grassy and shrub areas, especially close to water. They play a vital role in pinpointing concealed tigers, mainly through two kinds of alarm; one when a peafowl watches a tiger at close quarters and shrieks its warning, the other when a peafowl takes flight after a close brush with a tiger. These alarms are also sounded for jungle cats, jackals and birds of prey.

Twice when Laxmi and her cubs were walking through tall grass I saw one of the dominant cubs suddenly take off and leap into the long grass. On the second occasion this was followed by the shriek and death rattle of a peacock. I later had a fleeting glimpse of the cub as it bounded away, the peacock dangling from its mouth. On several occasions I have found the remains of a kill, with the exotic peacock feathers scattered all over the place. Even adult animals will pounce on, or swat, an unsuspecting peacock be it on the ground or on a low branch. The body contains two to three kilogrammes of meat and tigers must look on it as a tasty snack.

Young tigers regularly indulge in lying in wait for peafowl. Perhaps for them it is the first step in learning the art of killing and eating. I think the first kills that cubs successfully make are probably on peacocks, followed by langurs. Captain J. Forsyth in his book *The Highlands of Central India* (1872), states, 'The natives say that the tigress teaches her cubs to stalk and hunt by practising on monkeys and peafowls. The gorgeous plumage of the latter, scattered about in a thousand radiant fragments, often marks the spot where a peacock has thus fallen victim of these ready learners but the remains of a monkey are seldom or never seen.'

The peacock particularly fears the various members of the cat family and I remember one of the trackers telling me how he saw a jungle cat feeding on its peacock kill when a few minutes later a tiger strode along and bounded towards the cat, chasing it away and taking possession of the peacock which it proceeded to eat. Interaction between tiger and jungle cat is rare. Once, late in December 1984, while I was watching a tigress grooming herself, a jungle cat passed by some fifteen metres away with a mouse dangling from its mouth. It stood for a minute watching the tigress, tail wagging briefly, and strangely the tigress, fully alert, went into a crouch and the jungle cat moved off into the grass. The tigress then rose and walked around the edge of the thicket, peering carefully into the grass before returning to her original spot to continue grooming.

Fateh once saw Laxmi with a peacock kill. In the hot summer month of June, near the Lakarda water-hole, he spotted the tigress sitting by a bush.

THE HUNTED AND THE HUNTERS   149

The peacock has often been photographed displaying during his courtship ritual, but hardly ever has he been photographed fighting. Here, two males leap high in the air, kicking out at each other as they battle for the attentions of a nearby peahen.

ABOVE The tawny and grey coat of the jungle cat provides effective cover against the grass, leaves and leaf litter of the forest floor.

LEFT A jungle cat surveys the ground from her vantage point high in a tree. Peafowl are a favourite prey of this voracious little hunter, along with quail, partridges and mice.

RIGHT A peacock or peahen often provides the first 'personal' kill for a young tiger, but adults also take these forest birds whenever the opportunity arises. Here, Laxmi plucks the feathers from a cock bird, completely de-feathering the bird before eating the few kilogrammes of meat on it.

As he approached he saw a peacock lying beside her, partly eaten. She rose quickly and gripping the peacock just below the neck, carried it off into the thick of the bush. She then proceeded to de-feather it, spitting the feathers out before sinking her teeth into the flesh. It was an unusual sight. Some coloured feathers are often found in the faeces of tigers. I think the bird usually dies pinned under the forepaws or from a direct hit by a forepaw.

THE MINOR PREY SPECIES

The prey species discussed so far form the bulk of the tiger's diet. But there are several others. The cinkara or Indian gazelle is a petite and graceful antelope found in Ranthambhore in small numbers, usually on the open grasslands. Cinkaras are found in twos or threes, usually with one fawn. Males fight for the females during courtship but I have seen clashing males only once. These gazelles are light and exceedingly swift on their feet. I think a few fall prey to the leopard but in all these years in the Park only one leopard kill of a cinkara has been sighted.

We have never seen a cinkara killed by a tiger, or found the remains of one, and I feel that in Ranthambhore very few cinkaras die in this way. Their agility and swiftness probably facilitates their escape. However, on a couple of occasions their hairs have been found in the droppings of tigers. I once watched a pair of cinkaras who had spotted a tiger walking down the road.

BELOW The leopard is the second most powerful predator of the Ranthambhore forests, but it is no match for the tiger and avoids confrontation as much as possible. Leopards tend to hunt along cliff faces and hill-top terrain, especially at the forest edge. Because of the threat from the tiger, leopards are the most elusive of the Ranthambhore cats.

ABOVE A tiger scat consisting mainly of small bone fragments, the hair of the prey species and numerous broken porcupine quills.

Their alarm call — a spitting, hissing sound — went out immediately and with great leaps they disappeared over the crest of a hill. When they flee they leap so high off the ground they appear airborne. I think they can easily attain speeds of 80 to 100 kilometres per hour.

Another small prey species that tigers eat in Ranthambhore is the porcupine. These animals are scattered widely across India in open areas and grasslands, but actually live in the earth or in rock crevices. They are great excavators, and in Ranthambhore are almost totally nocturnal. They weigh 12 to 16 kilogrammes and can reach lengths of 80 to 90 centimetres. I have seen them rushing across the roads occasionally at night, but never in the day. They live generally on vegetables, fruits and roots and seem to have a good sense of smell. Porcupines defend themselves by charging backwards with their quills erect, often also making a strange grunting sound.

Fateh and I have on several occasions come across the scattered remnants of quills where a tiger has killed and eaten a porcupine, but I have never witnessed the kill itself. Despite the formidable quills, experienced tigers will aim to effect a clean kill by striking or biting the porcupine's head, its most vulnerable spot. But the quills are extremely sharp and can cause painful and even potentially fatal injuries to young and inexperienced tigers. If the quills get stuck in a tiger's paw he will try to pull them out. Often he will be successful and the wound will heal. But if they are deeply embedded, or if they are stuck in his neck, or mouth, or jaw where they cannot be reached, the wound may quickly turn septic. If this happens the tiger is in constant pain and his hunting ability is seriously affected. He is forced to look for easier targets than his normal prey and so may turn to cattle being grazed in the marginal parts of the forest. From there it is a small step to turning man-eater.

This happened quite frequently in the past. Jim Corbett describes the Mukteshwar tigress who was seriously injured in an encounter with a porcupine and soon turned man-eater, killing 24 people before she herself was killed. Dead tigers have been found in the past with quills embedded in the chest, paws, mouth, neck, throat and even in the back of the head. Corbett is said to have removed nearly 200 quills from the man-eaters he had shot, and some of these were up to 20 centimetres in length. The porcupine is no easy prey, but tigers continue to relish them.

Tigers also consume a variety of other birds and animals besides the soil and grass which they tend to munch with some regularity. Livestock like donkeys, goats, sheep and even camel are taken when opportunity presents itself. Ranthambhore has known several instances where tigers have attacked and eaten camels around the fringes of the forest. On very rare occasions they have been known to kill young elephants and rhinos and sometimes even bears and leopards. In Ranthambhore there have been a few cases of a tiger appropriating the kill of a leopard, but the leopard tends to keep away from the tiger and as tiger activity has increased in Ranthambhore, leopard activity has decreased. Sometimes I have not seen a leopard for over a year, and in 1982 we had 75 tiger sightings for every one of a leopard. Some records from early this century contain accounts of tigers killing and eating leopards, especially over their kills. Even recently in Corbett Park a tiger fought with, and killed, a leopard and proceeded to eat it. However, in Ranthambhore we have so far never come across such a fatal encounter.

The sloth bear is another large mammal that interacts with the tiger in Ranthambhore. The bears number about 100, in and around the Park, and are mainly nocturnal. They can stand the intense heat of summer and, unlike the Himalayan bear, do not hibernate in the winter. The sloth bear is about 90 centimetres in height, with a coarse brown-black coat and a pale V-shaped marking on the chest. The bear's curving claws are useful in digging up the earth and its exceptionally mobile lips are designed to suck insects and termites from crevices. On several occasions we have observed sloth bears digging frantically, sticking their heads into a hole and sucking insects out — often creating a small dust-storm in the process. Even a tree-pie disturbing this activity will be loudly grunted at. The bears' massive limbs with their inturned paws and long claws enable them to climb trees in search of fruit. I once saw a bear climb a ber tree and proceed, very clumsily, to shake the branches to dislodge the fruit. However, his shaky foothold forced him to give up, and after picking a few ber fruit from the ground he moved on. On another occasion one of our trackers found one bear up a tree, shaking down fruit, while a second bear was feasting down below.

Bears also eat carrion, and some of the interactions between tiger and bear arise over food. Corbett even recorded a Himalayan black bear chasing a tiger off its kill. In Ranthambhore the bear and the tiger tend to avoid each other as much as possible and only two fights have been recorded. In both, after a short boxing match, the bear gave way and was forced to flee.

A number of past records describe the tiger's prowess over the bear. In discussing a habitual bear killer, G. P. Sanderson states in his book *Thirteen Years Among the Wild Beasts of India* (1882), 'It appears that this tiger killed several bears at different times whilst feeding, coming up from behind and seizing them by the nape of the neck, and bearing them down (no pun intended) after a struggle, by his weight and strength.' F.C. Hicks, writing in 1910, records that, 'The whole thing was perfectly clear; after a prolonged fight the tiger had killed and eaten the bear – a thing which I had never known to occur before in all my experience.'

In China, Caldwell (1925) reported tigers eating pangolins. In Ranthambhore I have twice seen remnants of a monitor lizard in the scats of tigers. George Schaller, in his study in Kanha, once spotted a tigress sitting alertly in tall grass when suddenly she leapt high into the air to pounce on something, probably a rat or a mouse. In a similar situation in Ranthambhore a tigress was seen to leap into the air to attack a group of quail, and one of our trackers once glimpsed a young tiger bounding away with a partridge in its mouth. Observers over the last century have discovered an enormous range of food items in the tiger's diet – including snakes, turtles, lizards, crocodiles, frogs, fish and crabs, while George Schaller even found remains of winged termites and *Zizyphus* fruit in the droppings of a tiger. Frank Simpson, in *Sport in Eastern Bengal* (1886), wrote, 'I have proved

ABOVE A sloth bear clings to a precarious perch high in a ber tree, shaking the branches to dislodge the ripe fruits which form a major part of its diet. The bears of the Ranthambhore forest are shy and elusive animals and offer few opportunities for detailed observation.

RIGHT The Indian sloth bear shares many of the forest areas frequented by tigers, but the two species usually avoid each other. However, in direct confrontation the bear is usually the one to turn and flee, and there are well-documented cases of tigers that were habitual bear hunters.

. . . that they catch fish, turtles, crocodiles and large lizards. I believe they will occasionally eat sugar cane and maize; but the most curious thing I ever knew them to eat was grasshoppers. I once killed a tiger whose paunch was crammed full of grasshoppers or locusts.' The diet is indeed remarkably diverse and varied.

Tigers have also been known to eat tigers but I think that cannibalism is rare and probably happens only in desperate situations. Simpson, in *Sport in Eastern Bengal*, states, 'We followed the tracks in this direction and just as we entered this thick and difficult jungle we came on what seemed a fresh kill; to my astonishment, I saw the hind quarters of a tiger half eaten. . .'

────────────── THE TIGER'S KILLING TECHNIQUE ──────────────

The most relevant aspect of predation concerns the *way* in which the tiger kills. This has long been a controversial subject amongst sportsmen and naturalists in the past, and indeed remains so amongst observers of the tiger today. One of the most interesting early descriptions comes from Captain Thomas Williamson in his book *Oriental Field Sports* (1807). He writes, 'For I have already observed that the tiger is of all beasts of prey the most cowardly, its treacherous disposition induces it, almost without exception, to conceal itself until its prey may arrive within reach of its spring, be its victim either bulky or diminutive. Size seems to occasion no deviation in the tiger's system of attack, which is founded on the art of surprising. We find, accordingly, that such as happen to keep the opposite side of a road, by which they are somewhat beyond the first spring, often escape injury, the tiger being unwilling to be seen before he is felt. Hence it is rarely that a tiger pursues . . .

'The tiger's forepaw is the invariable engine of destruction. Most persons imagine that if a tiger were deprived of his claws and teeth he would be rendered harmless, but this is a gross error. The weight of the limb is the real cause of the mischief, for the talons are rarely extended when a tiger seizes. The operation is similar to that of a hammer, the tiger raising his paw, and bringing it down with such force as not only to stun a common sized bullock, or buffalo, but often crushing the bones of the skull.'

A.A. Dunbar Brander states, 'Few observers have been lucky enough to have seen an animal killed more than once or twice, and the circumstances may not have been the same as those witnessed by somebody else. The tiger is a most efficient engine of destruction and although he has his favourite methods even he has to vary these. I have seen tigers kill deer under natural conditions twice and bullocks in a herd three times.

'With regard to the deer and the loose bullocks, which were of course capable of moving, the tiger sprang up and in three short bounds had seized the neck. The animal had started into motion but the shock of the tiger's rush immediately rolled them over and the tiger hanging onto the neck twisted the same in the opposite direction to which the body of the animal was revolving. The weight of the revolving body opposed by the twist on the neck in the opposite direction resulted in instant dislocation.'

Richard Perry in his book *World of the Tiger* (1964), states, 'A tiger coming up to deer, which he has heard or winded, halts at the edge of the jungle and surveys the clearing where they are grazing. Then having ascertained their exact position he begins his stalk. With white belly trailing the ground and his great head, with jaw open and ears cocked, held very low he flows along with such stealth, placing each paw with infinite care, that the watcher must keep glancing to and fro between tiger and deer before he can ascertain that the former is in fact closing the distance between them.

'A number of observers have likened a stalking tiger to a brilliantly patterned giant snake, as with head extended so that chin and throat touch the ground, and every muscle seemingly strained, he propels himself along with amazing speed and absolutely no motion other than what appears to be a mere quivering of shoulders and hips.'

Jim Corbett saw some 20 kills of tigers and leopards in his time. In one of these a tiger made a head-on attack on a chital doe. Otherwise all the attacks

were from the rear or at an angle. Corbett once recorded an unusual encounter between a tiger and an adult buffalo. The tiger attacked a buffalo and leapt on to its back. The buffalo took off at full speed — with the tiger riding on its back. Eventually the buffalo shook the tiger off and escaped, but not before the tiger had eaten some two kilogrammes of flesh from its withers and five or six more from its hind quarters! The tiger's hunting prowess was vividly illustrated by Corbett when he recorded a pair of mating tigers who fought and killed a very large elephant tusker after a battle that lasted nearly the whole night. While one leapt on the elephant's back the other mauled its head in a two-pronged attack. It must have been an incredible feat.

Both Champion and Brander point out that the tiger sometimes kills by dislocating its victim's neck and at other times by strangulation. Hamstringing is a technique used against very big prey animals. The tiger will use its paws and canines to attack and disable the animal, by severing the tendon at the back of the hock. Only much later, once the animal is down, will the tiger attempt to grip it by the neck. Sometimes he is not successful. Brander states, 'I recall a typical case of a nilgai bull in which the tiger had fastened his left paw into the nilgai's ribs and had seized the buttock in his mouth. The strength of the bull had enabled him to break loose, and he got away with a deep score along his ribs and flank and about two pounds of meat and skin flapping on his hind quarters.'

Schaller, in 1964 in Kanha, found a freshly killed chital doe with a lacerated throat, tooth punctures on the lower back and claw marks on the chest. Another of his reports tells of an adult sambar stag apparently straddled by a tiger and severely lacerated before it managed to escape. Schaller found several deep scars on the animal's shoulders, side and rump.

F.W. Champion sums the art of killing well when he says, 'I don't intend to go into this subject any further but I think enough has been said to show that several methods of killing are employed by tigers according to the varying conditions of the individuality and age of the tiger, the size and kind of prey, and the circumstances in which the tiger gets an opportunity to seize it.'

Fateh and I have seen the tiger killing naturally on at least 30 occasions and we would generally agree with Champion's view, with the additional observation that the primary method is through a powerful wrenching grip on the vulnerable area of the neck.

The tiger is no doubt one of the most powerful predators that walks the earth, with an incredible versatility in feeding habit — from grass and grasshoppers to birds and fish, bears and elephants. The only animal to which the tiger itself has sometimes fallen prey in the past is the dhole or wild dog. Packs of over 20 dogs would surround a tiger and slowly tear it apart, even after losing several of their number to the tiger's powerful swipes. Today the wild dog is found only in small numbers, and large packs are extremely unusual. Man, with his gun, is the only other 'predator' to which the tiger falls victim.

Very rarely does a tiger die of disease. It normally lives out its full life span of approximately 20 years. Tigers that die earlier are probably killed by other tigers in conflict. I have never in all these years found the carcass of a naturally dead tiger. This mysterious predator seems to disappear without trace after death; elusive right to the end.

CHAPTER SIX

GENGHIS,
THE MASTER KILLER

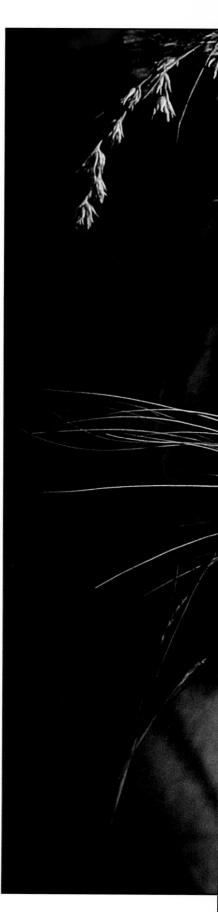

During 1984, Ranthambhore witnessed an extraordinary and quite exceptional form of tiger predation when one particular resident male developed a technique for attacking and killing his prey in the water, concentrating his activities around the three lakes. Nowhere in the literature of the past 200 years have we been able to find any other account of a tiger behaving in this way. As a strategist he is unmatched – an innovator. We called him Genghis, and this chapter is devoted to him.

Up to November 1982, as many as twelve tigers were using the limited area of the Ranthambhore lakes, their movement patterns overlapping constantly. But during the monsoon of 1983 a major change started to occur. A large prime male tiger was seen prowling about the area once or twice a month. By the end of August this had increased to nearly six times a month and he seemed to be asserting his dominance. Our sightings of the other tigers decreased proportionately. These were times of greatly increased vocalization between tigers, at night, and on two occasions there were sounds of vicious fights. During the winter months, between November 1983 and February 1984, Genghis became a regular visitor around the lakes and seemed to become more and more the dominant resident tiger. We now had only brief glimpses of the two adult tigresses who used the area occasionally. The rest had been pushed out.

Genghis enjoyed walking by the lakes in the mornings and late afternoons. But his behaviour was strange. He would stride along quite confidently, out in the open, not in the least bit bothered whether the deer spotted him or not. As soon as he was close to a group of deer he would break into a charge and chase them at full speed over distances of 100 to 200 metres. It was most unlike the normal hunting technique, in which the tiger would crouch, hide and stalk its prey. On these 'open walks' we twice observed Genghis killing a deer and carrying it off into thick cover to eat.

While he walked, Genghis indulged in regular spray-marking and 'flehmen'. He was obviously establishing territorial control by imprinting his own scent on the area – and especially over the markings of other tigers. Genghis must have marked over a hundred trees and bushes in the area. If he smelled the fresh presence of a tiger he would stand up on his hind legs near the tree and rake his forepaws over the area of the other tiger's spray. This activity was sometimes followed by a short period of strong vocalization. In fact, during the late evenings there were occasions when Genghis would walk right around the lakes vocalizing incessantly for over two hours in loud assertion of his claim over the area. Genghis was certainly an unusual tiger, and much more was going to happen.

Genghis appeared to have accepted the presence, around the area of the lakes, of the two females – one of which was almost certainly Noon. On the one occasion when he encountered a third female, he charged her, vocalizing

A close-up of Genghis, grimacing from behind a bush
during one of his first visits to the lakes area. He was a
magnificent male in the prime of life, some three metres in
length from nose to tail-tip and beautifully marked. His first
few weeks in the lakes area were spent entirely on asserting
his dominance.

viciously, and she rapidly disappeared from sight. Three times we saw Genghis strolling along the roads by the lakes followed at varying distances by 'Female No. 1' and 'Female No. 2', as they were designated at that time. The females would follow for a couple of hundred metres before branching off in different directions. Again, this activity is a kind of submission, with the females following the dominant male around his area. In such situations Genghis indulged in regular vocalization. In February 1984 he courted and mated with one of the females.

During these sightings we found that Genghis was fearless of human observers. He would quite happily walk in front of or behind our jeep. On one occasion a chital suddenly appeared to the right of him. Genghis chased the chital unsuccessfully for over 150 metres and at one point in the chase they missed the tyre of the jeep by only a couple of metres.

The seasons change by the end of February. The cold winter months are at an end and the onset of summer is just around the corner. This is a time when water dries up in the higher regions of the forest, and all the deer and antelope have to move down to the lower ground in search of it. The lakes become a critical source and the ungulates gather in large numbers around them. Their groups grow in size and as the heat increases the deer come frequently to drink. The sambar start immersing themselves in the water, grazing on lotus leaves, weeds and other water plants. The lakes suddenly throb with activity.

By early March Genghis was a regular feature there and on many occasions we found him camouflaged in the tall grass that surrounds the lake. On one such occasion a group of wild boar unsuspectingly approached him. In a flash he leapt and pounced on a piglet and swatted another with his paws. Carrying them one at a time he entered the grass to eat. We found him the next morning protecting the scraps of meat left over from his feast. He was exceedingly aggressive then and charged our jeep once, roaring in anger. By 11.00 a.m., after consuming the left-overs, he moved to Rajbagh where he went to sleep in the grass. A couple of hours later four sambar came around the edge of the lake and as they approached him he charged out of the grass, giving chase but unsuccessfully. He went back into the grass where he remained until sunset.

Late one morning a few days later we found Genghis walking towards Malik Talao where he disappeared into the tall grass. One whole side of the third lake was surrounded by these dense thickets, growing right down to the water's edge. We decided to spend the day watching the lake, and settled down, with our notebooks and camera equipment, in the cover of some bushes.

At 11.30 a.m. a group of four adult sambar approached along the lake shore. Immediately, Genghis popped his head out of the grass and started moving diagonally through it in the direction of the deer. Just as he reached the edge of the cover a peahen burst into flight nearby. Startled by the sound, one of the sambar turned — and spotted the tiger. As the deer started to stamp and bellow an alarm call, Genghis charged, but the bird had ruined his attack; the range was too great, and as the sambar leapt away, calling frantically, he broke off the charge and with an expression of annoyance padded slowly back into the cover of the grass thicket.

Despite the summer heat the lake was strangely quiet for much of the afternoon. A small herd of chital grazed on the far side of the lake; a few

RIGHT AND OVERLEAF This photo-sequence shows one of the first charges we saw Genghis make after his take-over of the Ranthambhore lakes area.

Genghis moved into this patch of long grass at about 11.30 a.m. after consuming the remains of a wild boar piglet he had killed the previous evening. He slept in the shade of the grass until 2.30 p.m., at which time a group of sambar appeared on the shore and started to move towards him.

As the sambar drew close, Genghis erupted from the grass in a headlong charge, scattering the deer in panic. The sambar flashed past our parked jeep and only at the last second did the charging tiger even see the vehicle. Slamming his forepaws into the earth he braked to a halt, then veered away snarling in frustration. At close range, head-on, the sheer power, strength and speed of his charge had been quite breath-taking.

RIGHT Malik Talao, 5.20 p.m.: Genghis stands motionless in the tall grass at the lake edge, deciding which of the sambar will be his main target.

BELOW Genghis has started his charge, rushing diagonally through the grass towards the sambar. The deer have seen him and with tails raised, calling in alarm, they flee farther out into the lake. It is just what Genghis wants. His diagonal run has cut off any chance of the sambar escaping onto the shore, and now they are forced into deeper water, confused and in total panic.

sambar entered the shallows, grazed a while, and then drifted away; but there was little activity in our immediate vicinity. A golden oriole chirped away on a nearby tree and a pair of paradise fly-catchers settled at the edge of the lake to drink. I had almost given up hope of the sambar returning. But then, just after 5.00 p.m., two groups of sambar appeared – approaching from opposite ends of the lake and wading steadily towards the centre, right opposite our observation point.

A slight movement stirred the tall grass at the far side of the lake where we knew Genghis lay hidden. A face appeared. He had moved right to the edge of the thicket and was peering out, studying the sambar with intense concentration. For several minutes he stood there, motionless, like a statue.

The next 30 minutes were some of the most tense and exciting I have ever lived through. Our sweating hands gripped our cameras and notebooks as we waited, with hearts thumping, for the tiger to make his move. With incredible patience Genghis waited, measuring the distance separating him from the sambar grazing peacefully in the water. And then he charged. In front of our furiously clicking cameras he crashed through the few remaining metres of long grass and plunged into the water. The lake seemed to erupt in an explosion of spray. Bounding through the water he made for a small

OVERLEAF With a mighty leap Genghis launches himself towards the waters of the lake. The sambar are frantically trying to flee but the weight of the water hampers their movements.

ABOVE Crashing through the water amidst sheets of spray, Genghis swerves towards his chosen target in an attempt to cut it off. His power and speed in the water is astonishing.

RIGHT A young fawn has been selected as the target of the attack. Its mother realizes and turns in anguish, knowing that there is little hope of survival for the fawn yet reluctant to desert her offspring.

ABOVE Genghis is now closing fast, pounding through the deep water with powerful strokes. The sambar hind rushes away: she has given up.

LEFT The end. The tiger's paw smashes down on the helpless fawn with such force that fawn and tiger disappear beneath the water. Only Genghis' tail is visible. This is one of the most remarkable pictures ever taken of the world's most powerful predator. Beneath the water the fawn is in its death throes as Genghis' canines close in a vice-like grip on its neck. The sambar hind watches in distress. A remarkable chase is over — one that has never before been seen, let alone recorded on film.

LEFT Genghis wades ashore, flicking water from his tail as he heads for the cover of the grass thicket to feed in privacy. The whole chase, from his emergence from the thicket to his disappearance back into it, has lasted barely two minutes.

Genghis charged the sambar in Malik Talao repeatedly, and with the remarkable success rate of one kill in every five attacks. But slowly the waters of the lake receded in the blistering summer heat. The strip of open ground between the lake and the tall grass became wider and wider — tilting the balance in favour of the sambar's escape. Realizing this, Genghis transferred his activities to Padam Talao.

group of hinds and their fawns, then changed his direction to concentrate his attack on one terrified fawn that had become separated from its mother in the panic. The young deer was doomed from that moment. Covering the last few metres with swift, powerful strokes, Genghis pounced — driving his victim under the surface then reappearing seconds later with the fawn's neck clenched in the killing grip.

We watched in amazement. Never before had we seen a tiger even attempt to launch an attack in the waters of the lake; nor was it something we had ever come across in old accounts. Was this just a temporary aberration or were we seeing something really new?

We left the lake at dusk in a state of elation. We had witnessed an astonishing feat, a successful hunt in water. Even better, we had captured the entire attack on film. Genghis was now making effective use of the area of

the lakes and utilizing it fully as a hunting ground. He had somehow managed to use the water to his own advantage, unlike the surprised sambar which had lost vital seconds watching the tiger bounding after it through the water. The camouflage of the tall grass was perfect. Genghis was almost showing off. He was even ready to attack the sambar after having killed and eaten only a few hours earlier. And this was not just an unusual day. Genghis spent 24 days between the second week of March and the second week of April using the same strategy in Malik Talao. He killed six young sambar. This strategy was obviously effective on the younger animals who seemed to lose precious time in their confusion. But the summer heat was increasing and the water level in Malik Talao was dropping rapidly. By early April there was a wide gap between the grass and the water and Genghis' success was diminishing. He now had to cover quite a distance on dry land

Padam Talao is a much larger
lake than Malik Talao and
Genghis had to adapt his
hunting technique to take
account of the deeper water and
the sambars' greater choice of
entry and exit points. Instead of
charging straight into the water
he would rush along the shore
in full view of the sambar,
throwing them into a panic. As
the deer made a frantic dash for
one of the exit points, Genghis
would charge along the shore,
sometimes for 150m or more,
to attack them in the shallows
as they tried to scramble
ashore. In this sequence he
makes an unsuccessful attack
near one of the exit points.

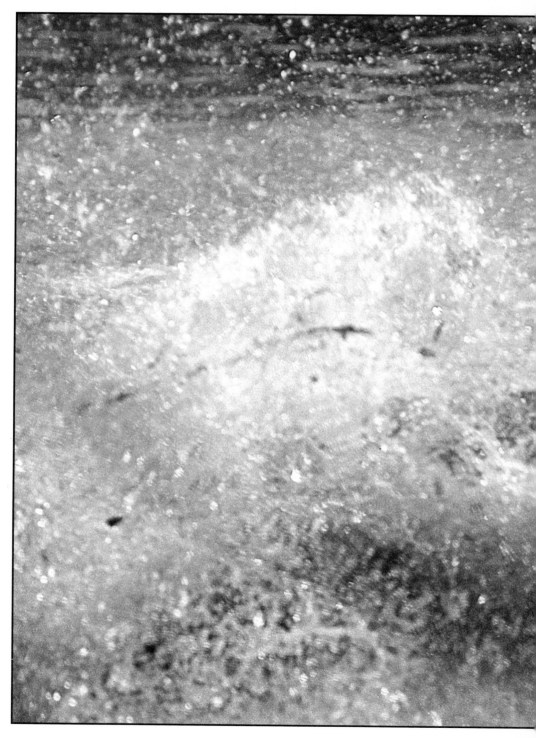

before hitting the water, and the sambar had more time in which to make their escape. In the second week of April we witnessed one of the last successful kills that Genghis made in Malik Talao.

In response to the changing situation, Genghis switched his activities to Padam Talao – still using his new strategy of attacking in the water. Padam Talao was much larger than Malik Talao and on most of its shoreline there was still the cover of tall grass thickets. Naturally we followed, and soon discovered that the best vantage point from which to observe the attacks was Jogi Mahal itself, which is located on the edge of the lake. Besides charging into the water to kill, Genghis also tried two other strategies. In the first he would see a group of sambar from the grass and then come right up to the edge of the water, out in the open, to watch them – causing the sambar to bolt in alarm. As this lake is large it is not possible for the sambar to cross from one side to the other with ease. Instead, they invariably bolted towards the corners, and Genghis would attempt to cut off these exits and make his kill as the deer fled from the lake. To do this he sometimes had to run nearly 150 metres, which at full pelt is an amazing feat and one that invited comparison with the technique of the cheetah. His other strategy was to swim out into the lake, pursuing groups of sambar with powerful strokes and causing much confusion. If, in this process, a single animal got separated, Genghis would overpower it with ease. He seemed to patrol all sides of the lake, constantly watching the entry and exit points. Sometimes in the terrible heat of the afternoon he would spot a group of sambar in one corner and then stalk them for some 200 metres before going into a charge. If there was a jeep on the road watching the scene he would stalk around the jeep, moving with it and using it as a cover for his final ambush.

But Genghis' hunting forays into the water were not without problems. Padam Talao had some 60 marsh crocodiles and as Genghis was killing in the water he came into aggressive conflict with the larger ones. On one such occasion he was found sitting at the edge of the lake looking carefully at a spot in the water. He sat for several hours watching, as crocodiles splashed and nibbled around what must have been the carcass of a sambar. Twice he swam back and attacked the spot where he thought there was a carcass, but in vain. On the third occasion he went back into the water and in great fury smashed at the water with his forepaws. Dipping his head down he quickly grabbed the carcass, and made for shore. He had to swim at least 45 metres and still managed to keep a grip on the carcass – which was of an adult sambar hind. While swimming he wrapped a paw around the sambar's neck and used the other paw to stroke the water. Once, for a moment, he disappeared under the water with the carcass but quickly surfaced again and powerfully stroked his way to dry land. An amazing feat. A tiger swimming to shore with an animal weighing at least 200 kilogrammes.

This struggle for food under the water must have been something to watch. The crocodiles must have pulled with all their might but Genghis' paws were more powerful. He came back wet and exhausted, but victorious. On other occasions when he found a crocodile he would snarl and grimace at it viciously. Since he spent long periods of time around the lakes he was annexing the kills of the crocodiles, and the carcasses of animals that had died of natural causes which the crocodiles had pulled from the shore into the lake.

For two days in the middle of April Genghis courted and copulated with 'Female No. 2'. She was the more regular in his presence and was the one we called Noon. Monitoring her we found that she had not conceived after this mating, and she was still without cubs a year later. Apart from this courtship activity Genghis spent most of his time stalking Padam Talao. He used every strategy in the book, be it on dry land or in water. He had one particular bush in which he ate and to which he carried all his kills. It was like a graveyard.

By the end of April Genghis was also using Rajbagh as a hunting ground. Here he sought the thick cover of lotus flowers for his swim after the sambar, and though we never saw a kill on this lake he must have had a high rate of success. He would spend most of the night strolling by the lakes, taking up a position before dawn in anticipation of a sambar entry or exit.

Genghis' use of the lakes as a regular hunting ground naturally brought him into frequent conflict with the resident crocodiles, especially through his habit of scavenging their kills. Here, with one paw raised aggressively, Genghis moves towards a crocodile partly immersed in the shallows. Normally the two species would not interact.

The day was spent sleeping in the grass and waiting for the deer to come down to the lake. His activity seemed more diurnal and exactly the opposite of what had once been regarded as normal nocturnal activity. One of his shelters was a deserted lake palace between Padam Talao and Rajbagh where he would spend much time resting in its cool confines.

From the end of April to the end of May he spent 24 days on Padam Talao. This is unusual as most male tigers do not remain in one spot but cover large distances in their forest. Genghis had obviously decided that the lakes were ideal hunting grounds and therefore the question of disappearing for days did not even arise. Since early March we had seen 18 natural kills. But by the beginning of June the lakes were drying up rapidly and the gaps between grass and water were widening. Genghis was no longer seen regularly. He was moving off into other areas and was now visible around the lakes only once every three or four days.

Interestingly, his preference in predation also seemed to shift – from sambar in the water to chital on the shore. One of the reasons for this was related to the widening gap between grass and water, which made successful predation in water increasingly difficult. As the chital would gather on the shore to graze on the green grass, Genghis shifted his attacks to them. By the middle of June, temperatures in the forest hover around 45° Centigrade and Genghis would spend much of his time soaking in the water at the edges of the lake, and if he were eating in the grass he would come to drink and sit in the water at least four or five times during the day. At this time of year water becomes a vital factor for the whole life cycle of a forest. We were amazed at the levels of energy that Genghis had displayed throughout the summer months. But this had changed by June, and though occasionally he indulged in half-hearted charges, most of the time this kind of hectic activity was far too enervating in the blistering heat.

As the presence of Genghis became more irregular around the lakes we realized that another season was starting, and that the activity that had

When Genghis failed to reappear after the rains in 1984, it seemed as though we had seen the last of his remarkable charging activity. But to our delight it soon became apparent that Noon, Genghis' companion during part of the previous year, had learned from him. Here she makes one of her first charges towards sambar feeding in the lake. She was hesitant, not even bothering to follow through into the water when the deer began to flee. But it was a start.

fascinated us for nearly four months was now at an end. The whole forest had been burnt dry by the sun and all eyes were on the sky waiting for the rains to explode. And they did, in early July. After the first showers all the water-holes and crevices in the higher regions became sources of water, and no longer were the deer and antelope forced to congregate around the lakes. Only small groups of animals were scattered about. Genghis and his sport in water would have to wait for the start of another dry season, the following March. Would Genghis be able to keep his hold in this prime hunting area or would he be pushed out by another male? We would have to wait several months for the answer to that question.

The character of Genghis was unique compared with the other tigers we had observed. For the first time we were looking into the complexities of the thinking mind of the tiger. Fearless and independent, Genghis had evolved as part of the new generation since the tiger was afforded special protection in 1973. He was a tactical planner and he employed a strategy that made him an expert and master killer. His gradual take-over of the area of the lakes, and his perfect technique in using water to advantage in predation, set

him apart from other tigers. We had a feeling, however, that other tigers would follow his example, and that the next season would reveal even more remarkable developments.

Genghis was also quite aggressive. When eating he would not tolerate humans anywhere near him. On other occasions he would use human presence to his own advantage, either by stalking with a jeep as cover or by allowing the noise of an approaching jeep to cover the sound of his movements through the grass. He did not tolerate any other tigers in the area besides the two females. Nor any other large animals. And he was exceedingly aggressive with crocodiles. On one occasion an unknowing sloth bear approached a bush which sheltered Genghis. Immediately he leapt out and attacked the bear, slapping it with his paws. The bear used his forelegs to retaliate but in seconds had turned and loped away into the thicker forest. Genghis seemed to have an in-built hostility towards one and all. But he was usually even-tempered with us and our jeep, and the only time he threatened to attack us was when we came too close to him while he was eating. We had certainly developed a bond of some sort. But this relationship ended when, after October 1984, Genghis was no longer seen. A new male tiger, Kublai, had taken over the area of the lakes. He was as large as Genghis, and in perfect condition. As the months rolled on and there was no further sign of Genghis I felt sad and depressed and wondered where he had gone. Had Kublai battled with him? Kublai was a dry-land killer, never attempting to enter the water in pursuit. His behaviour pattern differed sharply from that of Genghis.

Noon was the resident tigress and after Genghis' departure she became his *alter ego* so far as killing in the water was concerned. She was the one who was in regular contact with Genghis while he was around, and had even mated with him. She had obviously watched and learnt from him the art of killing in water. From November 1984 to February 1985 Noon's forays into the water seemed hesitant and lacked Genghis' expertise. She seemed to give up her charge after a certain point. Once, late in January, she raced into the water after a group of sambar. Most managed to flee, but two helpless young fawns remained and then moved in panic into deep water. Noon watched them alertly but instead of rushing in to grab them she retreated into the grass. In such a situation, Genghis would have killed one of the fawns in a flash. Noon had a lot to learn, but she was trying.

By the end of February I had seen her charge seven times in the water, and all she had managed to kill was one sambar fawn, caught at the edge of the water late one evening. But between the beginning of March and the middle of April, Noon's forays into the water became more regular. The onset of the summer was early, with water drying up rapidly in the hilly areas of the forest. Large herds of sambar started appearing around the lakes and moving in to feed on the succulent plants that grow in the water. I always find the sambar's addiction to water amazing. They seem to pass this habit on to their young, and in complete disregard of the threat of predators they just pour into the lakes in the summer to feed. In March the influx was in full swing and Noon's predation started to develop and improve, just like Genghis' in the previous year. Between 1 March and 8 April of 1985, Noon killed six sambar fawns in the water. I saw her charge unsuccessfully on some 20 occasions. During this month her strategy developed rapidly, and for the first time I noticed Genghis' technique emerging in her.

I remember one hot afternoon in March when Noon charged into the water from the grass, missing a sambar by inches. She walked back into the grass. An hour later another group of sambar entered the water about 100 metres from her. In typical Genghis fashion she immediately stalked the distance through grass. It was the first time I had seen her move from a fixed position, taking the risk, like Genghis had done regularly. She erupted from the grass and splashed into the water — but again the sambar managed to evade her. Normally she would have given up at this point but instead she ran back to the shore and up an incline in an effort to cut off the sambar's exit point. Again she was unsuccessful, but her strategy was developing.

Late the same evening she charged another group of sambar at the far

corner of the lake and on this occasion she was able to leap on the back of a fawn, bringing it down and killing it by sinking her canines into the nape of its neck. She quickly dragged it out of the water and into a thick bush 100 metres or so from the shore.

On another occasion she left the cover of high grass at Rajbagh one evening, moving towards a group of sambar about 70 metres away. The first 15 metres was covered in a stealthy walk, and then quite suddenly she broke into a lightning charge, covering the remaining distance in seconds and nosing towards a young sambar which she successfully brought down. Clamping her canines firmly into its neck she carried it back to the high grass to feast on. Similar activity was sustained throughout the month and she seemed to have become a really close second to Genghis, the master killer.

Summer arrived unusually early in 1985, and by the middle of April charging activity was at its lowest ebb. The heat was intense, and this combined with the widening gap between grass and water made it impossible for Noon to sustain her hectic activity. I think that beyond a certain temperature it becomes impossible for a tiger to pursue prey over long distances. Genghis to some extent was an exception, and though only irregularly he continued this exhausting activity into May and June.

Kublai, although regular in his presence around the lakes, never

ABOVE A few weeks after her first hesitant attempts, Noon thunders into the waters of the lake with a power and determination worthy of her teacher. The photograph was taken by Günter from the far side of the lake.

RIGHT At the same time, Fateh was photographing the charge from close quarters, hidden in the lakeside vegetation near Noon's point of attack. Having selected a young sambar hind as her target, Noon is just about to make her final lunge when a large splash of water hits her in the face, temporarily blinding her. The moment's hesitation is just enough. The hind gains a metre or so and her feet touch firm ground on the lake bed. Before Noon can regain the initiative the sambar is accelerating towards the beach — and safety. This time Noon missed — but day by day her success rate was improving.

LEFT Kublai, the dominant male who took over the lakes area from Genghis, lies on a high ruined wall carefully watching Noon making her first charging attempts at the far side of the lake. At first, Kublai showed a strong dislike of the water, but he followed Noon's activities very closely. This picture was taken in March – and in the first week of May I witnessed Kublai's first, rather clumsy, attempt to charge into the water. He was learning from Noon. The technique had not been lost with Genghis' departure: far from it, his successors were actively exploring it for themselves.

BELOW Noon was also forced into conflicts with crocodiles through her activities in and around the lakes. Here, having just annexed the rotting remains of a sambar stag she pauses to snarl in anger at the frustrated reptiles watching her from the water.

attempted to charge the sambar in the water. It seemed alien to his experience, his instinct and his nature. Curiously though, he remained in close touch with Noon and I remember him twice spending the whole day on one side of the lake, carefully observing Noon on the other and especially her charging activity in the water. Would he eventually start emulating her, as she had emulated Genghis? For the moment he seemed quite happy as the resident male tiger, annexing most of Noon's sambar kills in the water. Each time she killed she had only a few hours in which to eat alone before Kublai arrived and seized the carcass. Noon would sit endlessly after that, waiting to be invited to the feast. But in vain. Only once did I see her actually whisking the carcass away while Kublai was taking a drink.

At the end of April Kublai was seen regularly. He appeared to have torn the pad of his left forepaw, causing him to walk with a pronounced limp, but fortunately by 4 May it was healing rapidly. On this day I jumped for joy as it was the first time I saw Kublai charge. He had been resting under a mango tree and in the early afternoon he walked stealthily out of the grass and towards a bunch of six sambar some 45 metres away. The first 20 metres of his walk in the open went unnoticed by the sambar, but as soon as he was spotted a sambar hind bellowed in alarm and Kublai broke into a clumsy but fairly fast charge. The sambar escaped, and Kublai sank into the water to cool off. I was delighted. He might just become the lake charger of '86. He had obviously learnt something from Noon. He was able to brave the heat of the afternoon and charge through the lake, even with a slight injury.

Noon was now a confirmed lake predator, and like Genghis she was forced to interact with the crocodiles who scavenge the naturally dead animals by the shore. The crocodiles have a tough time tearing up a carcass, and after much watching and waiting, which sometimes lasted a full day, Noon would choose her moment and rush into the water, annexing the carcass from the crocodiles. On one occasion, after two days of the crocodiles being unable to consume a large sambar stag, despite its putrefied

and bloated state, Noon dragged the stinking carcass more than 100 metres towards a patch of grass, watched by a group of crocodiles in the water. She paused several times for breath, and to snarl at the crocodiles. While dragging it a small part broke away from the main body but Noon ignored this and disappeared into the grass. A short while later she emerged, backed towards the shore, immersed her tail in the water and then flicked it repeatedly, thereby spraying herself all over. She did this for some 15 minutes before returning into the grass.

On another occasion a large chital stag was found dead on the shore of Rajbagh. In the evening some Egyptian and white-backed vultures came down to feast on the carcass. The vultures fought for supremacy and one of them, with wings flapping, stood on the carcass doing a typical 'goose dance', thereby asserting its dominance. Then they went for the meat; but this was no easy process. The carcass was relatively intact and, apart from the natural openings, it was difficult for the vultures to feed. They attempted to tear out bits and pieces amidst much flapping and fighting.

LEFT Still watched by the crocodiles, Noon walks backwards along the lake shore, dragging the stinking carcass towards a patch of tall grass.

RIGHT Having hidden the carcass in a tall grass thicket, Noon returns to the lakeside to cool herself. Letting her tail slide into the water she then flicks it over her back — splashing and spraying herself with cool water. We had never before seen a tiger use its tail in this way.

Launching itself out of the water, a large dominant crocodile chases off a smaller one attempting to feed from the carcass of a sambar hind (on which a number of large frogs can be seen). Aggressive interactions are a common feature of crocodile feeding behaviour and it is astonishing just how fast these large reptiles can move in the water. In the coming years the relationships between tiger, deer and crocodiles around the Ranthambhore lakes will provide a marvellous opportunity to study the dynamic changes of an evolving ecosystem.

Suddenly several sambar alarms rang out as a large crocodile glided towards the carcass. The vultures beat a hasty retreat. The crocodile clamped his jaws firmly on the rump of the chital, chewed off a bit, and then made an effort to drag the carcass into the water. Several other crocodiles watched from a distance. We moved closer but the crocodile shied away and moved back to the water. The vultures rushed back to the carcass. It was dusk and we left. The next morning we discovered that Noon had successfully stolen the carcass from the crocodiles and had dragged it into a bank of tall grass.

Noon seemed a little more wary of the crocodiles than Genghis had been, and on one occasion a large crocodile foiled her attempt to annex a carcass by lashing his tail towards her, forcing her to retreat. Most of the time she was successful, but even after taking a kill from the crocodiles, Kublai would promptly turn up and grab the carcass from her. She would accept this. They both always snarled viciously at passing crocodiles in the water, emphasizing this relationship of competition and conflict.

In deep water the crocodile is able to kill young sambars by gripping them by the mouth as they drink and then dragging them into the water where they

ABOVE Rolling on to its side, with one foot clear of the water, a crocodile attacks a school of small fish near the edge of Rajbagh. Fish form the staple diet of the lake crocodiles and this individual is making the most of a good feeding opportunity. All around him, egrets wait in anticipation, hoping to snatch any fish driven towards them by the crocodile.

drown. This, however, seldom happens in the Ranthambhore lakes as the water is not very deep. Here, the victims are normally sambar fawns, especially ones that have strayed into the shallow waters. The crocodiles' teeth are not sharp and they try with desperation to break open the carcass. They tend to have problems especially with large animals that they may have scavenged, and are often forced to wait for the carcass to bloat and putrefy before they are able to puncture it. This can take a full day or even two. They seem unable to tear the hide of an animal that has been freshly killed. And because of this time-lag Noon would spot the carcass and annex it during her regular lake beat.

Because they are 'cold blooded' animals, with a normal body temperature of about 26°C, crocodiles take every available opportunity to bask in the sun on the shores of the lakes. This is particularly important to them in the winter months when prolonged cold makes them sluggish and lethargic. The need for energy-giving warmth also explains why, especially in winter, they must wait for a carcass to become rotten, and consequently much easier to dismember.

When feeding, the crocodiles in these lakes seem to have a clear 'pecking' order. The larger and more dominant ones chase the younger crocodiles away from the carcass, and force them to wait at the edges. I have several times seen two large crocodiles streaking through the water towards each other and amidst much splashing they seem to push at each other with tail and jaw until the less dominant one leaves the fray.

Once firmly established in possession, the dominant crocodile remains with a carcass to protect it from intruders. He expends a good deal of energy in the initial task of opening up the carcass, but then has new problems: as soon as he starts eating, all the other crocodiles attempt to join in the feast and there is often much fighting and pulling at the remains. The crocodile's jaws are designed for gripping, not severing, and pieces of the carcass are wrenched off with a violent twisting motion deriving its power from the massive tail. Then the crocodile has to rise to the surface in order to swallow. The animal's digestive system is extremely efficient. Everything but hair is digested, and that is formed into a compact ball which is later regurgitated.

One thing has now become very clear in Ranthambhore: as a direct result of the tigers' change to diurnal habits and their increasing use of the lakes as a killing ground, they are now coming into direct competition with crocodiles and are interacting with some regularity. There are few records in the past of such encounters. It has been noted that crocodiles are sometimes able to drown young tiger cubs that venture into the water, but very seldom in India have they managed to cope successfully with an adult tiger. In an aggressive encounter it is the occasional slash of the tail that sometimes forces a tiger to retreat. And this only from large-sized crocodiles.

Colonel Kesri Singh describes an unusual crocodile-tiger interaction that took place in 1921 on the shores of the Chambal River near the forest of Ranthambhore. As far as I know it is one of the very few descriptions of such an encounter. One night, Kesri Singh heard a great splashing and commotion in the river and thought that it was a pair of crocodiles mating. But the next morning the carcass of a three-metre-long crocodile was found floating nearby. Careful examination revealed several deep lacerations on the crocodile, especially on the belly, and then to his astonishment Kesri Singh found a piece of a tiger's tail clamped in the crocodile's jaws. Later he discovered that while crossing the river a tiger had fought off and killed a crocodile – losing part of his tail in the process!

In recent years the crocodiles of the Ranthambhore lakes seem to have increased quite significantly in size, and it seems likely that as the years pass they will become more and more serious predators on the water-loving sambar. Crocodiles of even two or three metres length are capable of attacking and killing small animals, and larger crocodiles will almost certainly prefer these large mammals to their more usual diet of fish. For students of Ranthambhore's forest life, and her tigers in particular, the next few years should provide a wealth of interest. If the innovative hunting technique pioneered by Genghis and followed by Noon and to a lesser extent by Kublai becomes more widely adopted (and who better to pass it on than a tigress, the teacher of the next generation?) then interaction between tiger and crocodile can only increase. And what of the long-term future? Will the combination of tiger and crocodile eventually prove too much for the sambar and force them to seek new summer feeding grounds? And if that happens, what of the tigers?

LEFT Crocodiles continue to grow throughout their lives, and Rajbagh has several measuring 3m and three or four measuring 4m. Crocodiles of this size can take quite large animals, and in addition to snatching occasional fawns the lake reptiles are now beginning to attack adult sambar. It is a remarkable new development. In this photograph a large crocodile glides round a sambar hind looking for a place to gain a firm hold. The deer is paralysed with fear. She has already lost one ear, and even though she eventually escaped onto the shore she died a day later from shock and her injuries.

THE FUTURE

But what of the tigers of tomorrow? Will they have an opportunity to co-exist with man into the twenty-first century? In 1973, when 'Project Tiger' started, the world population of tigers was just under 4,000. In 1985 the figures should be about 7,500, a much healthier picture. There are many reasons for this increase.

In recent years there has been a growing awareness and sensitivity towards the tiger and its habitat. India today has 15 specially designated 'Project Tiger' reserves stretching right across the country. It also has 57 National Parks and 243 wildlife sanctuaries covering 14 different types of forest. In Nepal, conservation measures have been adopted in the Chitawan National Park, and in two other reserves, Karnali and Sukla Phanta, in the western part of the country. The Indonesian government set up the Meru-Beriti Game Reserve at the same time as 'Project Tiger' to protect the very small number of Javan tigers. The Sumatran government followed suit with the vast Gunung Leuser Reserve and the Malayan government set up a reserve in the state of Trengganu to protect the Indo-Chinese tiger. Thailand also has four reserves, the National Park at Khao Noi and three other sanctuaries in the region of the Khawae Noi river system. The Soviet Union has had some success with the Siberian tiger in the Sikhote Alin Reserve, the Suputinsk Reserve and the Lavaski Reserve. Even in China a serious effort is at last under way to protect the tiger in a variety of different provinces. The Chang-bai Shan Reserve, the Mengyan Reserve and the Fangjinshan Reserve are just three of the many protected habitats.

But will the tigers that are born today survive? A difficult question. I fear that problems for the future of the tiger and its habitat are increasing sharply and will shortly loom large over the species' future. The reasons are many, and to understand them at any reasonable depth we must look at India, the country with the largest and most viable population of tigers, and at Ranthambhore, a microcosm of this world effort to save the tiger.

In 1984 the official figure for the tiger population in India was around 4,000, an increase over the previous decade of 2,200. And even though the methodology behind tiger counting is not very convincing, the last decade has certainly shown marked progress. The margin of error in such counts could well be between 25 and 35 percent and is due partly to the problems of using pug marks as the identifying factor and partly because the tiger is too elusive and evasive to be counted with any degree of accuracy within a period of a few days. The count of tigers in National Parks and 'Project Tiger' reserves numbers some 1,500. The rest, the majority, live outside any such protective umbrella and in areas where controls are less rigorous. Their

A scene whose loss to the world would be unthinkable.
A mature tigress, Nick Ear, wades through the shallow
waters of Rajbagh watched by a small herd of nervous sambar.
The still lake, surrounded by forest and the ancient
ruins of palaces and temples, is the setting for a marvellous
success story – the recovery of the Ranthambhore tigers.
Today they are safe. But their continued survival into the next
century is by no means assured. The survival of the
world's most magnificent predator rests in the hands of man.

future is much more uncertain, and today one wonders whether it will ever be possible to preserve that future against the wanton destruction of the tigers' natural habitats.

Ranthambhore, which is one of the smallest 'Project Tiger' reserves, exists under the umbrella of special rules and guidelines. After a decade of protection, tiger activity within the Park seemed to reach a peak in 1984 – the population having increased from 14 tigers to 40 between the 1973 and 1984 census counts. But after the monsoon of that year there was a gradual, and very worrying, decline in the frequency of sightings.

The major problems facing the tiger are related to people and their livestock. The villagers around Ranthambhore depend directly on livestock for their livelihood, be it milk from the cattle or cash from the sale of goats. The mild monsoon showers of 1984 created an acute shortage of fodder and so tremendous pressure was exerted right around the Park by man and cattle. From September 1984 to February 1985 the incessant activity of cattle graziers and grass-cutters was recorded by the Park staff. It was all illegal, and had not been witnessed in the previous years. The villagers seemed desperate, taking grave risks in order to collect grass for fodder, even negotiating almost inaccessible gorges and stream beds.

Under this kind of pressure the effective patrol and control of 400 square kilometres of forest is almost impossible. It was a tough task for the forest guards. Many people were caught and many cattle were impounded, but the damage had already been done. Because of this incessant human activity the normal life cycle of the forest had been severely disturbed. Aggressive man, on foot, was now damaging the natural habitat and not only interacting with the tiger, but also impinging on the normal activities of deer, antelope and countless other species. On one occasion in 1984 I followed a tigress into a dry stream bed and found her confronted by a large group of grass-cutters, who with much shouting and waving managed to scare her away. Imagine her consternation at this encounter with man – a situation her memory might well have recorded with indelible clarity. The tiger is not stupid. It may have taken a decade for it to shed its nocturnal cloak, but just a few such episodes could so easily see it donned again.

And these escalating levels of conflict have now spilled over into the relations between the Park staff and the people of the surrounding villages. Despite all attempts to employ tact and persuasion to relieve the pressures imposed by human intrusion into the Park, there have been violent incidents. The worst of these occurred in August 1985 when a forest patrol came under a barrage of rocks and boulders thrown by a band of illegal graziers. One forester was killed and several of his companions were seriously injured.

Many parts of India are being crippled by problems and 90 percent of them are being caused by man. But is it possible for a country of 730 million people to protect and save its rich and varied natural heritage against the combined onslaught of industrialization, modernization and the tradition of keeping livestock? Nearly 1,000 million livestock exist in India today. They are found in every natural habitat and consume vast amounts of vegetation of all kinds. With major increases in population and livestock, what would be the fate of the already depleted eight percent of the country's forest cover? Are we going to denude ourselves of nature's mantle and rot in the depths of uncontrolled pollution? This year, 1986, is going to be critical. It might see success in wildlife protection but could all too easily see the beginnings of a decline. We seem to be walking across a tightrope – tottering at several points and not knowing when we might take the plunge downwards.

Our future is now directly related to man, his livestock and their impact on India's remaining wilderness areas. The future of such areas is therefore in the hands of the villagers who ring these forests. This fact above all must be appreciated by national and international, official and non-official, organizations concerned with saving wildlife. Let us not build dreams and wrap ourselves in the comfortable cocoons of success stories. The harsh reality must be faced, and immediate action – at local level – is needed to secure the future of wildlife.

Ranthambhore today is surrounded by 10,000 to 15,000 people with some 40,000 head of livestock. There is incredible pressure on the fringes and buffer zones of the Park: almost every blade of grass has been stripped away. To prevent the devastation of grass-cutting, wood-felling, grazing and poaching, a series of socio-economic developmental measures must be implemented as a matter of the utmost urgency. People must be removed from the areas of conflict – but in a way sensitive to their immediate and long-term needs and aspirations.

Organizations like the WWF must begin a serious effort to disseminate their activities and educational programmes into rural areas. They could, in fact, set up a chain of educational units throughout India, and they must concentrate on opening offices in small towns rather than in the large cities.

A second factor concerns forest corridors and adjoining forest belts. Because of intensive grazing on the fringe areas of the Park, most of the forest corridors that formerly connected Ranthambhore with the adjoining forest belts have slowly been eroded away, leaving wide open gaps and forcing the Park into isolation, like an island. This is not the most healthy situation for the wild inhabitants within, be they deer, pigs or tigers. As interaction between tigers increases they tend to come into conflict. This is one of the primary methods of keeping their population in check. But this conflict can cause serious injury to some of the animals, forcing them to depend on the livestock freely available in and around the forest margins. This in turn inevitably brings them into direct conflict with man, and can lead to the first tendencies among tigers towards man-eating. It is therefore important to expand the boundaries of the Park and regenerate the forest corridors into adjoining areas.

This is an operation requiring large amounts of financial support. Ranthambhore has three adjoining forest belts, the Kualji Reserve, the Sawai Man Singh Sanctuary and the Kela Devi Sanctuary. At the moment all efforts are concentrated on bringing these areas under the umbrella of 'Project Tiger'. As soon as that is achieved it will be necessary to regenerate the forest corridors into these areas and translocate even more villages out of them and into more appropriate agricultural belts. If such an operation is successful it will inject a new lease of life into the area, providing a much more extensive habitat and for the tigers the possibility of increased movement and reduced conflict. I think this will also go a long way towards sustaining a viable genetic pool for future generations of tigers as a larger area will to some extent reduce the possibilities of in-breeding. But to effect such a massive expansion programme the support of the people who live in the area is vital, and this support and approval can only come if the action plan of socio-economic development is immediately implemented.

Even if Ranthambhore does become an island, the tigers themselves will almost certainly work out a way to keep their population in check, and this is a process that requires detailed research and observation. But if the population exceeds the optimum level unchecked, and some of the tigers take to extreme fringe areas, attacking livestock and occasionally man, then they must be carefully identified photographically and a process set in motion to cull them scientifically. Personally I am against the culling of tigers and feel that such a method should be used only against proven and dangerous man-eaters. In fact before we start culling tigers we should seriously consider culling some of the vast numbers of cattle and other livestock that are such a serious drain on our natural resources.

So far the man-eating problem has not reached serious proportions. In Ranthambhore there have been no cases at all in the last decade. Throughout India the known cases amount to some 50 fatalities every year, with most of the deaths due to accidental encounters – in two particular areas. The first is the Sundarbans in West Bengal and the second is the Tarai belt of Uttar Pradesh which borders Nepal. Both areas have their own specific problems. In the Sundarbans the mangrove swamps are dense and inaccessible. Many villagers enter these areas on foot to collect forest produce, especially honey. Visibility is down to a few metres and because of this people are bound to fall victim to the tiger. This activity has been going on for decades and some of the tigers must have passed on the man-eating habit to their offspring. There is a definite solution to the problem. It is possible to provide alternative sources of livelihood for these people, and this should be a job for the Forest Department. Uncontrolled entry into such a difficult habitat on foot must of course be banned. The problems will then decline.

In Lakhimpur Kheri on the Indo-Nepalese border there has been tremendous encroachment into forest belts by sugar cane cultivators. This factor has caused conflict between tiger and man. Many a tigress takes shelter in such cane fields because they are dense and form useful protection for their cubs. When disturbed by the cultivators they attack to protect their cubs, and gradually a normal animal can turn into a man-eater. Again it is a situation where sugar cane cultivation must be moved out of the forests. These farmers must be given new subsidies with possibilities of new land for cultivation in agricultural belts, out of the forest. If this is not done, how can one blame a tiger for turning its aggression on the human intruder?

There are, of course, several other important measures that need to be taken, including better policies for recruitment into the wildlife service, staff welfare measures, strict tourism controls, better research facilities, the commencement of several major research projects and, finally, greater budgetary allocations. But before we even think of going into such detail let us concentrate all our efforts for the moment on the villagers without whose support no forest can ever survive. Their economic development, as stated before, is a critical step towards the serious conservation of our flora and fauna. Let us all, nationally and internationally, put our heads together and initiate a series of action plans all over India to stabilize the rapidly deteriorating situation and secure the future of our wilds and of that super-predator, the tiger. Ranthambhore has evolved from the Maharaja of Jaipur's hunting reserve to a sanctuary, then to a 'Project Tiger' reserve and finally a National Park. Today it is being considered for inclusion in the World Heritage list. It is one of the world's great treasures, and like some others requires careful handling at national and international levels.

Most Indians have a deep-rooted acceptance of nature and animals and this has been passed down for countless generations in myth, legend and religion. We have, over the centuries, developed an in-built sensitivity to nature and its conservation. Nature is only destroyed when man's survival is at stake. So let us ensure the survival of both with care and determination, as one cannot live in isolation from, or neglect of, the other.

Kublai, currently dominant male of the Ranthambhore lakes area, framed in a gateway of the old lake palace.

THE EVOLUTION AND CURRENT STATUS OF THE TIGER

The origin of the big cats is a subject of much debate, but the group as a whole are the descendants of the miacids – small insect-eating mammals that flourished more than 50 million years ago. Sabre-toothed cats of various forms appear in the fossil records of Eurasia and North America nearly 40 million years ago but it is now generally accepted that the tiger in its present form probably originated in Siberia. Our earliest fossil remains of this 'modern' sabre-tooth come from the Chigar caves of the New Siberian Islands. These impressive cats became extinct some 10,000 years ago but by then their descendants, the true tigers, had begun to extend their range – forced to spread southwards in search of suitable habitats as successive phases of the Ice Ages made northern Asia uninhabitable. Tigers were well documented in the ancient Hindu Vedic scriptures and had probably arrived in the subcontinent about 5,000 B.C. Today, the range of the tiger stretches several thousand kilometres across Asia from Siberia to the China Sea and southeastwards into the Malay Peninsula.

The modern tiger (*Panthera tigris*) comprises eight subspecies, the largest being the Siberian tiger, measuring up to 3.9m, while the smallest, the island subspecies of Java and Sumatra, rarely exceed 2.7m from nose to tail-tip.

THE SIBERIAN TIGER (*P. t. altaica*) is the largest, heaviest and most powerful of the subspecies. It has a thick, furry coat to withstand the extreme cold and can weigh up to 320 kilogrammes. In the Soviet Far East it survives in pockets of the Amur valley and the upper reaches of the Khor and Bilkin rivers. The present population in the Soviet Union is around 250. A small population of this subspecies also survives in northeastern China. The exact population figure is not available but it might be over 100.

THE CHINESE TIGER (*P. t. amoyensis*) is a smaller tiger with a shorter coat than the Siberian and much broader striping. (The fur is, however, much longer than that of the Indian race.) Small numbers might exist still in parts of China – in southern Szechwan and the province of Fukien and the Yangtse River Valley. It has been rarely seen recently in the wild and its numbers are unknown.

THE INDO-CHINESE TIGER (*P. t. corbetti*) is found in China in the southern parts of Yunan, Kwangsi and Kwantung provinces. It also has a large range stretching from southern China and eastern Burma to Vietnam and the Malay Peninsula. Compared with many subspecies its numbers are quite healthy at between 1,500 and 2,000.

THE SUMATRAN TIGER (*P. t. sumatrae*), found only on the island of Sumatra, is small and more fully striped than the Indo-Chinese tiger. It is found in the northern part of the island and the mountainous regions in the south-west. Again its population is smaller than that of the Indo-Chinese tiger; possibly between 500 and 800.

THE JAVAN TIGER (*P. t. sondaica*) is another of the smaller subspecies and has a darker ground colour. Its status is critical, being probably extinct or on the verge of extinction.

THE CASPIAN TIGER (*P. t. virgata*) is a medium-sized tiger with closely striped fur, originally occupying a huge range from the Caspian eastward through northern Iran and Afghanistan and north to the Aral Sea and the Irtish Basin. It is almost certainly extinct.

THE BALI TIGER (*P. t. balica*) was already rare at the turn of the century and is now extinct. The last one was reported to have been shot in 1937.

THE INDIAN TIGER (*P. t. tigris*) has the largest population today and its range extends over most of India, Nepal, Bhutan and western Burma, where it merges with the Indo-Chinese race. Averaging about 2.7m in length, the male can weigh 180-250 kilogrammes and the female 135 kilogrammes. This subspecies is very adaptable, coping with extremes in temperature from 0°C to 47°C in some parts of India. It therefore has a relatively short but glossy coat. Its total population is estimated at 4,000.

Thus, taking all the subspecies into account, the total known population of the tiger as a species is between 6,000 and 7,500. Allowing for the imperfections of census methods, most authorities accept a figure of 7,000.

Tigers have proved extremely adaptable to variations in temperature and habitat. In Manchuria they are found in deep snow, at temperatures of –34°C, and in a habitat of birch, scrub oak and walnut thickets. In China they shelter in coniferous forests and high grass thickets, tamarisk and cork forests, and even marshes and reed beds. In India they are found at temperatures of 47°C in dry deciduous and evergreen forests; in mangrove swamps like the Sundarbans; and in the Himalayan foothills between Nepal and Sikkim at altitudes of nearly 3,700m. They are also found in the rainforests of Indo-China, Burma and Malaya, the mangrove swamps of Sumatra, and the grass thickets of Kampuchea and Thailand. They are also thought to survive still in pockets in Vietnam, even after the devastation of war.

IDENTIFYING AND COUNTING TIGERS

Identifying tigers is a complex art. Some naturalists believe that the tiger's pug mark is much like a fingerprint, unique to each individual. However, in Ranthambhore we have never had much success in pin-pointing the identity of a tiger by this method. In my experience the only time a pug mark is useful is when the tiger's pad or claw suffers from some deformity that shows clearly and consistently in each print.

The most important criterion in identifying tigers is for the observer to have a sound understanding of tiger behaviour and habits. Tigers, like human beings, have different characters and individual likes and dislikes, and vary tremendously in their behaviour patterns, especially from one forest to another. To identify them requires a thorough understanding of the areas they live in and their movement patterns. Observers should also understand the overlapping movements of other tigers in the area, and keep a day-to-day record of the happenings in an area.

The only foolproof method of identifying a tiger is through a photographic record of the individual's face and profiles. Every tiger has slightly different markings and these do not change during its life. In Ranthambhore we have managed to photograph and identify 24 tigers in this way, and each tiger has been given a name for easy reference. Sometimes the stripes on the body can also assist identification, but a thorough knowledge of the facial markings is critical. Unfortunately the photographic method is not universally practicable. Unlike Ranthambhore, which is a dry, open, deciduous habitat, most tiger habitats are thicker and relatively inaccessible, with limited visibility. In these areas, tigers cannot be identified individually with accuracy.

Population counts are made in an annual census operation at the height of the summer when there are limited water-holes and tiger movement is restricted. Over 5,000 people take part and the operation is based on collecting plaster of Paris casts and traced impressions of the tigers' pug marks around water-holes, *nallahs*, animal paths and man-made roads. Each impression is marked clearly according to the place and time at which it was found, and then sent on for analysis by the research staff of the forest.

A tiger can walk more than 20 kilometres in a night and on a variety of different soils, thereby leaving impressions that to the layman look quite different. Sometimes, even though only one tiger has walked an area it can appear as if six tigers have passed by. For such a census operation the forest is divided into blocks; each one checked by two or more forest guards. Sometimes a tiger will have walked through ten blocks, leaving a variety of impressions depending on the soil. In such situations ten casts of his pug marks may go to a base point for tabulation. The problems in accuracy are therefore immense, and invariably the margins of error are high.

The pug mark method of counting can only be successful when every forest tracker and guard is highly motivated, very knowledgeable and experienced in the census area to which he is assigned, fully trained in the recognition and analysis of the pug marks of all the forest animals, and totally familiar with the day-to-day activities and movements of tigers within his area of forest. But this is too much to expect. Recruitment into the forest service is not based on a man's interest in the tiger, or in wildlife. The forest guard joins because he has to earn a livelihood. Census operations are therefore treated casually and with little respect and consequently suffer from large margins of error.

RANTHAMBHORE: A SELECTED SPECIES LIST

The 400km² forest of Ranthambhore supports a rich and varied flora and fauna including at least 450 named plant species. The bird list for the National Park has 272 species; the mammal list has 22. There are a dozen or so reptiles and amphibians and a profusion of insect life. The list here provides the common and scientific names of the main species that feature in the text of this book.

MAMMALS
Tiger *Panthera tigris*
Leopard *Panthera pardus*
Jungle Cat *Felis chaus*
Indian Porcupine *Hystrix indica*
Small Indian Mongoose *Herpestes edwardsii*
Striped Hyena *Hyaena hyaena*
Jackal *Canis aureus*
Sloth Bear *Melursus ursinus*
Wild Boar *Sus scrofa*
Spotted Deer (Chital) *Axis axis*
Sambar *Cervus unicolor*
Indian Gazelle (Cinkara) *Gazella gazella*
Blue Bull (Nilgai) *Boselaphus tragocamelus*
Common (Hanuman) Langur *Presbytis entellus*

REPTILES
Indian Marsh Crocodile *Crocodilus palustris*
Indian Monitor Lizard *Varanus griseus*
Soft-shelled Turtle *Trionyx gangeticus*

BIRDS
Grey Heron *Ardea cinerea*
Purple Heron *Ardea purpurea*
Pond Heron *Ardeola grayii*
Large Egret *Ardea alba*
Painted Stork *Mycteria leucocephala*
Greylag Goose *Anser anser*
Crested Hawk-Eagle *Spizaetus cirrhatus*
Bonelli's Eagle *Hieraaetus fasciatus*
Crested Serpent Eagle *Spilornis cheela*
King Vulture *Sarcogyps calvus*
White-backed Vulture *Gyps bengalensis*
Egyptian Vulture *Neophron percnopterus*
Grey Partridge *Francolinus pondicerianus*
Peafowl *Pavo cristatus*
Red-wattled Lapwing *Vanellus indicus*
Brown Fishing Owl *Bubo zeylonensis*
Pied Kingfisher *Ceryle rudis*
Small Blue Kingfisher *Alcedo atthis*
Stork-billed Kingfisher *Pelargopsis capensis*
White-breasted Kingfisher *Halcyon smyrnensis*
Golden-backed Woodpecker *Dinopium benghalense*
Golden Oriole *Oriolus oriolus*
Pied Myna *Sturnus contra*
Common Myna *Acridotheres tristis*
Tree-pie *Dendrocitta vagabunda*
Jungle Crow *Corvus macrorhynchos*

Any reader wishing to know more about the work being carried out at Ranthambhore, or wishing to visit the reserve, should write direct to the Field Director, 'Project Tiger', Sawai Madhopur, Rajasthan, India.

TIGER LITERATURE

The following selected bibliography includes all those accounts to which reference is made in the text, and from which passages have been quoted, plus a range of books both old and new which the reader may find interesting and informative.

AFLALO, F.G.A. *The Sportsman's Book for India* (London, 1904)
 A Book of the Wilderness and Jungle (London, 1926)
ALI, S. The Moghul emperors of India, as naturalists and sportsmen. *Journal of the Bombay Natural History Society* **31(4)**: 833-61 (1927)
ALLEN, H. *The Lonely Tiger* (London, 1960)
ALVI and RAHMAM. *Jahangir – the Naturalist* (Delhi, 1968)
ANDERSON, K. *Nine Man-eaters and One Rogue* (Allen & Unwin, 1954)
 Man-eaters and Jungle Killers (Allen & Unwin, 1957)
 The Call of the Man-eater (Allen & Unwin, 1961)
 The Tiger Roars (Allen & Unwin, 1962)
 This is the Jungle (Allen & Unwin, 1967)
BAIKOV, N.A. *The Manchurian Tiger* (Hutchinson, London, 1925)
BAILLIE, W.W. *Days and Nights of Shikar* (London, 1921)
BAKER, E.B. *Sport in Bengal* (Ledger Smith & Co., London, 1886)
BAKER, E.C.S. *Mishni the Man-eater* (London, 1928)
BAKER, S. *Wild Beasts and their Ways* (London, 1890)
BALDWIN, J.H. *The Large and Small Game of Bengal and the North-western Provinces of India* (1877)
BARRAS, J. *India and Tiger Hunting* (London, 1885)
BAXTER, E.H. *From Shikar and Safari* (London, 1931)
BAZÉ, W. *Tiger, Tiger* (London, 1957)
BEATSON, A. *A View of the Origin and Conduct of the War with Tippoo Sultan* (Nicol, London, 1800)
BEST, J.W. *Tiger Days* (London, 1931)
 Indian Shikar Notes (London, 1931)
 The Marked Maneater (London, 1934)
 Forest Life in India (London, 1935)
BISCOE, W. A tiger killing a panther. *Journal of the Bombay Natural History Society* **9(4)**: 490 (1895)
BLANDFORD, W.T. *Fauna of British India* (London, 1891)
BLANE. *Prince's Sports* (London, 1800)
BOSWELL, K. 'Scent trails' and 'Pooking' in tigers. *Journal of the Bombay Natural History Society* **54(2)**: 452-54 (1957)
BRADDON, E. *Thirty Years of Shikar* (London, 1895)
BRADLEY, M.H. *Trailing the Tiger* (London, 1930)
BRANDER, A.A. DUNBAR. *Wild Animals in Central India* (Edward Arnold, London, 1923)
BROOKE, V. *Big Game in India* (1894)
BROWN, J.M. *Shikar Sketches: With Notes on Indian Field Sports* (1887)
BURKE, R.ST.G. *Jungle Days* (London, 1935)
BURKE, W.S. *The Indian Field Shikar Book* (London, 1920)
BURTON, E.F. *Reminiscences of Sport in India* (London, 1885)
BURTON, R.G. *Sport and Wildlife in the Deccan* (London, 1928)
 The Book of the Tiger. (London, 1933)
 A Book of Man-eaters (London, 1936)
 The Tiger Hunters (London, 1936)
 The tiger's method of making a 'kill'. *Journal of the Bombay Natural History Society* **49(3)**: 538-41 (1934)

BUTT, K.S.J. *Shikar* (London, 1963)
CALDWELL, H.R. *Blue Tiger* (London, 1925)
CAMPBELL, T. A tiger eating a bear. *Journal of the Bombay Natural History Society* **9(1)**: 101 (1894)
CARR, N. *Return to the Wild* (London, 1962)
CHAMPION, F.W. *With Camera in Tiger Land* (Chatto & Windus, London, 1927)
 The Jungle in Sunlight and Shadow (Chatto & Windus, London, 1933)
CONNELL, W. Wild dogs attacking a Tiger. *Journal of the Bombay Natural History Society* **44(3)**: 468-70 (1944)
COOCH BEHAR, MAHARAJA. *37 years of Big Game Shooting* (Bombay, 1908)
CORBETT, G. A tiger attacking elephants. *Journal of the Bombay Natural History Society* **(7)1**: 192 (1892)
CORBETT, J. *Man Eaters of Kumaon* (Oxford Univ. Press, Oxford, 1944)
 The Temple Tiger (Oxford Univ. Press, Oxford, 1952)
 My India (Oxford Univ. Press, Oxford, 1952)
 Jungle Lore (Oxford Univ. Press, Oxford, 1953)
COURTNEY, N. *The Tiger, Symbol of Freedom* (London, 1980)
CUMINGHAM, A.H. *Indian Shikar Notes* (1920)
DAVIES, D. *Tiger Slayer by Order* (London, 1916)
DAMSON, G.A.R. *Nilgiri Shooting Reminiscences* (1880)
DHARMAKUMARSINHJI, K. *A Field Guide to Big Game Census in India* I.B.W.L. Leaflet no.2 (1959)
EARDLEY-WILMOT, E. *Forest Life and Sport in India* (Edward Arnold, London, 1910)
 The Life of a Tiger (London, 1911)
 Leaves from an Indian Forest (1920)
'EHA'. *A Naturalist on the Prowl in the Jungle* (London, 1894)
ELLISON, B.C. *The Prince of Wales' Sport in India* (London, 1925)
FAYRER, J. *The Royal Tiger of Bengal* (London, 1875)
'FELIX'. *Recollections of a Bison and Tiger Hunter* (London, 1906)
FEND, W. *Die Tiger von Abutschmar* (Zurich, 1972)
FENTON, L. Tigers hamstringing their prey before killing. *Journal of the Bombay Natural History Society* **(4):756** (1905)
 The Rifle in India (London, 1923)
 The Forests of India (London)
FIELD, D.M. *Jungle Jottings 1908-1928* (Jodhpur Govt. Press 1936; London, 1936)
FIFE-COOKSON, J.C. *Tiger Shooting in the Doon and Alwar* (London, 1887)
FLETCHER, F.W.F. *Sport on the Nilgiris* (London, 1911)
FORSYTH, J. *The Highlands of Central India* (London, 1872; Chapman & Hall, London, 1919)
GEE, E.P. *The Wildlife of India* (Collins, London, 1964)
GHORPADE, M.Y. *Sunlight and Shadows* (London, 1983)
GLASFURD, A.I.R. *Leaves from an Indian Jungle* (1903)
 Rifle and Romance in the Indian Jungle (London, 1905)
 Musings of an Old Shikari (London, 1928)
GORDON-CUMMING, R.G. *Wild Men and Wild Beasts* (London, 1872)
GOULDSBURY, C.E. *Tiger Land* (London, 1913)
HANLEY, P. *Tiger Trails in Assam* (Robert Hale, London, 1961)
HEARSEY, L. Tiger Killing Swamp Deer or Gond. *Journal of*

the *Bombay Natural History Society* **35(4)**: 885-86 (1932)

HEWITT, J. *Jungle Trails in Northern India* (Methuen, London, 1938)

HICKS, F.C. *Forty Years Among the Wild Animals of India* (Pioneer Press, Allahabad, 1910)

HORNADAY, W.T. *Two years in the Jungle* (Kegan Paul, Trench & Co., London, 1885)

HOSE, C. *Fieldbook of a Jungle Wallah* (London, 1929)

INGLIS, J. *Tent Life in Tiger Land* (London, 1888)
    Sport and Work on the Nepal Frontier (London, 1892)

ISMAIL, M.M. *Call of the Tiger* (1964)

IYER, K.B. *Animals in Indian Sculpture* (Bombay, 1977)

JADHO, K.R.B.S. *A Guide to Tiger Shooting* (London)

JEPSON, S. *Big Game Encounters* (London, 1936)

JERDON, T.C. *Mammals of India* (London, 1874)

JOHNSON, D. *Indian Field Sports* (London, 1827)

KHAN, I. Association between a leopard and a tigress. *Journal of the Bombay Natural History Society* **39(1)**: 155-6 (1936)

KHAN, S.A.S. *Shikar Events* (London, 1935)
    Wild Life and Hunting (Delhi, 1978)

KINLOCH, A.A. *Large Game Shooting in Tibet and the North West* (London, 1876)

KRISHNAN, M. *India's Wildlife in 1959-70* (Bombay, 1975)

LARKING, C. *Bundobust and Khabar Reminiscences of India* (1888)

LEVESON, H.S. *The Forest and Field* (London, 1874)
    Nilgiri Sporting Reminiscences (London, 1880)

LEWIS, E. The Sambar call of the tiger and its explanation. *Journal of the Bombay Natural History Society* **41(4)**: 889-90 (1940)

LITTLEDALE, H. Bears being eaten by tigers. *Journal of the Bombay Natural History Society* **4(4)**: 316 (1889)

LOCKE, A. *The Tigers of Trengganu* (London, 1954)

LYDEKKAR, R. *A Hand-Book to the Carnivora* (Edward Lloyd Ltd., London, 1896)
    The Game Animals of India (London, 1924)

MCDOUGAL, C. *The Face of the Tiger* (Rivington Books, London, 1977)

MOCKLER-FERRYMAN, A.F. *The Life-Story of a Tiger* (London, 1910)

MORRIS, J. *Winter in Nepal* (London, 1963)

MORRIS, R. A tigress with five cubs. *Journal of the Bombay Natural History Society* **31(3)**: 810-11 (1927)

MOUNTFORT, G. *Tigers* (London, 1973)
    Back from the Brink (London, 1978)
    Saving the Tiger (London, 1981)

MUNDY, A. *Pen and Pencil Sketches* (John Murray, London, 1833)

MUSSELWHITE, A. *Behind the Lens in Tiger Land* (London, 1933)

OKEDEN, W.P. *Diary and Sporting Journal of India: 1821-41* (London, 1906)

PERRY, R. *The World of the Tiger* (Cassell & Co. Ltd., London, 1964)

PIGOT, R. *Twenty-five Years Big Game Hunting* (London, 1928)

POCOCK, R.I. Tigers. *Journal of the Bombay Natural History Society* **33(3)**: 505-41 (1929)
    The Fauna of British India: Mammalia (London, 1939)

POLLOCK, F.T. *Fifty Years' Reminiscences of India* (London, 1896)
    Sports in British Burma (London, 1900)
    Sporting Days in Southern India (London, 1903)

POWELL, A.N.W. *The Call of the Tiger* (London, 1957)

PRATER, S.H. *The Wild Animals of the Indian Empire* (Madras, 1934)

RATHORE, SINGH and THAPAR *With Tigers in the Wild* (Vikas Publishing, Delhi, 1983)

RICE, W. *Tiger Shooting in India* (Smith, Elder & Co., London, 1857)
    Indian Game (London, 1859)

RICHARDSON, W. Tiger Cubs. *Journal of the Bombay Natural History Society* **5(2)**: 191 (1890)

RUSSELL, C. *Bullet and Shot in Indian Forest, Plain and Hill* (London, 1900)

SAHARIA, V.B. *Wildlife in India* (Delhi, 1982)

SANDERSON, G.P. *Thirteen Years Among the Wild Beasts of India* (W.H. Allen & Co., London, 1882)

SANKHALA, K. *Tiger* (Collins, London, 1978)

SAVORY, I. *A Sportswoman in India* (1906)

SCHALLER, G. *The Deer and the Tiger* (University of Chicago Press, 1967)

SESHADRI, B. *The Twilight of India's Wild Life* (John Baker, London, 1969)

SHAHI, S.P. *Backs to the Wall* (Delhi, 1977)

SHAKESPEAR, H. *Wild Sports of India* (London, 1862)

SHEFFIELD, F. *How I Killed the Tiger* (London, 1902)

SHEHAN. *A Guide to Shikar in the Nilgiris* (London, 1924)

SIMPSON, F.B. *Letters on Sport in Eastern Bengal* (London, 1886)

SINGH, A. *Tiger Haven* (London, 1973)
    Tara, a Tigress (London, 1981)
    Tiger Tiger (Jonathan Cape, London, 1984)

SINGH, K. *The Tiger of Rajasthan* (London, 1959)
    Hints on Tiger Shooting (The Hindustan Times Ltd., Delhi, 1965)

SINHA, R.K. *Purnea, a Shikar Land* (London, 1916)

SIVARAMAMURTI, C. *Birds and Animals in Indian Sculpture* (Delhi, 1974)

SMEETON, M. *A Taste of the Hills* (Rupert Hart-Davis, London, 1961)

SMITH, A.M. *Sport and Adventure in the Indian Jungle* (London, 1904)

STEBBING, E.P. *Jungle By-ways in India* (London, 1911)
    The Diary of a Sportsman Naturalist in India (The Bodley Head, London, 1920)

STERNDALE, R.A. *Natural History of Indian Mammals* (London, 1884)

STEWART, A.E. *Tiger and other Game* (London, 1927)

STOCKLEY, C.H. *Big Game Shooting in the Indian Empire* (London, 1928)

STRACEY, P.D. *Tigers* (London, 1968)

STRACHAN, A.W. *Mauled by a Tiger* (London, 1933)

SUTTON, R.L. *Tiger Trails in Southern Asia* (London, 1926)

SUCKSDORFF, A.B. *Tiger in Sight* (Andre Deutsch, London, 1965)

TAYLOR, M.L. *The Tiger's Claw* (London, 1956)

TODD, W.H. *Tiger! Tiger!* (London, 1927)

TOOGOOD, C. Number of cubs in a tigress' litter. *Journal of the Bombay Natural History Society* **39(1)**: 158 (1936)

TRENCH, P. *Tiger Hunting, A Day's Sport in the East* (London, 1836)

TURNER, J.E.C. *Man-eaters and Memories* (London, 1959)

VAIDHYA, S. *Ahead Lies the Jungle* (London, 1958)

WARDROP, A.E. *Days and Nights with Indian Big Game* (London, 1923)

WEBBER, T.W. *The Forests of Upper India* (London, 1902)

WILLIAMSON, T. *Oriental Field Sports* (Orme, London, 1807)

WOODYATT, N. *My Sporting Memories* (Herbert Jenkins Ltd., London, 1923)

WRAY, J.W. *With Rifle and Spear in India* (London, 1925)

INDEX

ACKNOWLEDGEMENTS

The author acknowledges the use of some extracts from his writings that have been published in *The India Magazine* and *Sanctuary Magazine*.

The author also acknowledges Vikas Publishing House (New Delhi) for the use of extracts and paraphrased extracts of his writings in their publication *With Tigers in the Wild* (1983) by Fateh Singh Rathore, Tejbir Singh and Valmik Thapar.

Eddison Sadd acknowledgements:
Creative Director Nick Eddison
Editorial Director Ian Jackson
Editors Martyn Bramwell and Charlotte Edwards
Designer Nigel Partridge
Proof Reader and Indexer Jackie Pinhey
Cartographic Editor Caroline Simpson
Map Artist Andrew Farmer
Production Bob Towell

The photographs in this book were taken by:

Günter Ziesler 6-7, 9, 17, 19, 20-21, 22-3, 24, 24-5, 26-7, 28-9, 32-3, 35, 36(BR), 38-9, 40-1, 43(2), 44-5, 45, 49, 50(C), 51(2), 52-3, 54-5, 56-7, 58, 60(2), 60-1, 68-9, 69, 76-7, 78, 80-1, 82-3, 86(T), 88-9, 93, 94-5, 97, 98, 98-9, 100-1, 102-3, 104(B), 105(2), 106, 106-7, 108-9, 110-11, 112, 113, 114-15, 116-17, 122-3, 123, 130, 130-1, 132(T), 136, 136-7, 138, 138-9, 141, 142-3, 144, 145, 148-9, 149, 150, 151(T), 153(T), 154, 154-5, 158-9, 160-1, 162-3, 163(2), 164, 164-5, 166-7, 168, 168-9, 169(3), 170-1, 172-3(B), 176-7, 178-9, 180, 181, 182, 183, 184-5 (Günter Ziesler's photographs appear here by arrangement with Bruce Coleman Limited.)

Fateh Singh Rathore 2, 12, 29, 31, 36(L), 36(TR), 50(T&B), 53(R,2), 62(2), 63, 64(2), 65(2), 66-7, 72(2), 73, 80(B), 84(T&B), 90, 91, 96, 110(L), 118, 120, 121, 122(T&L), 125(T&B), 126, 127, 132(B), 134(T), 135(T), 151(B), 152-3(B), 172(T,3), 173(T,3), 175, 179(R,3), 186, 187, 193

Valmik Thapar 85, 86(B), 102(T), 104(T), 125(C), 134-5(B), 146(2)

Tejbir Singh 10-11, 26, 46, 188-9